D0444454

From Zero to Eternity
in 60 Seconds Flat

Influencing Others
for Christ at a
Moment's Notice

Wendell Smith

Charisma®
HOUSE
A STRANG COMPANY

Most STRANG COMMUNICATIONS/CHARISMA HOUSE/SILOAM
products are available at special quantity discounts for bulk
purchase for sales promotions, premiums, fund-raising, and
educational needs. For details, write Strang Communications/
Charisma House/Siloam, 600 Rinehart Road, Lake Mary,
Florida 32746, or telephone (407) 333-0600.

FROM ZERO TO ETERNITY IN 60 SECONDS FLAT
by Wendell Smith
Published by Charisma House
A Strang Company
600 Rinehart Road
Lake Mary, Florida 32746
www.charismahouse.com

Unless otherwise noted, all Scripture quotations are from the
New King James Version of the Bible. Copyright © 1979, 1980,
1982, Thomas Nelson, Inc., publishers. Used by permission.

Scripture quotations marked KJV are from the King James
Version of the Bible.

Scripture quotations marked NIV are taken from The Holy
Bible, New International Version. Copyright © 1973, 1978,
1984, International Bible Society. Used by permission.

Cover design by Mark Labbe

Library of Congress Cataloging-in-Publication Data

Smith, Wendell, 1950-

From zero to eternity in 60 seconds flat / Wendell Smith.
    p. cm.
 Includes bibliographical references.
 ISBN 1-59185-466-0 (pbk.)
 1. Witness bearing (Christianity) 2. Evangelistic work. I. Title.
 BV4520.S53 2004
 248'.5--dc22

                              2004005869

AUTHOR'S NOTE: For added emphasis, I have used italics for certain words and phrases in Scripture quotations.

04 05 06 07 08 — 987654321
Printed in the United States of America

Dedication

THIS BOOK IS dedicated to several evangelists I have known and admired for their bold witness.

To Dr. Bill Bright, the greatest personal soul-winner of our time—who befriended and blessed me in an extraordinary fashion in the final year of his life.

To Dr. Billy Graham, who inspired us all every time we heard him declare, "The Bible says..."

To Dr. Luis Palau, Reinhard Bonnke, and Dr. T. L. Osborne—some of the great crusade preachers of the gospel of Jesus Christ.

To Dr. Marilyn Hickey, a leader among the host of women who proclaim the good news.

To Francis Anfuso, Gary Beasley, Marc Estes,

Dr. Mark Jones, and other exceptional evangelists in local churches.

To Dr. Dick Iverson, my father in the faith, who modeled evangelization and discipleship in the local church as we trained under his ministry in Portland, Oregon, for so many years.

And to many evangelists in our church in Seattle—Becky Fouquier, Sharon Altig-Smith, Dave Soleim, Jennifer Kraker, Fred Kropp, Jim Tehero, Dave Heindel, Joel Pike, Amy Benthin, and so many others.

And I dedicate this book also to my son, Judah Elwood Smith; to my son-in-law, Rev. Benny Perez; to my sister-in-law, Pastor Tami McKinney (who could win anybody to Christ); to an old friend, Rick Olsen (who always believed everybody liked him); and to my grandson, B. J. Perez, and the future evangelists of his generation.

Contents

Foreword

OVER THE YEARS, I have asked millions of people what they considered to be the two greatest privileges in life. I personally consider the two greatest privileges in life to be having a relationship with Jesus Christ and leading a lost person to salvation through that same relationship.

Although I have known many pastors in my lifetime, I can truly say that I have been deeply impressed with the Spirit-filled leadership of Reverend Wendell Smith, senior pastor of The City Church in Seattle, Washington. God is using him to touch his city and his world.

As a pastor of a "growing-and-going" church, Pastor Smith is cultivating dynamic leadership principles in the lives of his people, in his inner circle of influence in the great Northwest, and now in the world at large. And in this book, he shows us the pathway to powerful Christian living and church growth.

For more than fifty-five years, I have measured the value of everything I have done against whether or not it helped me to fulfill the Great Commission. If it did not help me to fulfill the Great Commission, then I simply did not do it. I admire leaders who share this same desire—the desire to see disciples made for the Lord Jesus. I believe this new and unique book will become an invaluable tool to soulwinners, pastors, evangelists, and believers who want to make a difference in their generation and help usher in the age of the return of Christ.

How does a believer witness to a lost person when he has only a moment or two of contact with that person? As you know, we live in a fast-paced society—all of us have so much to do every day. Pastor Smith provides an unusual approach to accomplishing the Great Commission when you only have a few moments of contact with an unbeliever. His fresh, dynamic approach supplies the dedicated Christian with an arsenal of words, phrases, and ideas for sharing the claims of Christ in those daily divine encounters that we all experience.

Through this book, believers will learn a new technique for taking advantage of those significant moments that come their way. People all around us are standing at the crossroads of life—they are truly the "multitudes in the valley of decision." Many are searching for truth and looking for something solid on which they can build their lives.

Are you taking full advantage of the two greatest privileges in life? Would you like to become more effective in winning the lost to Christ? You hold in your hands a powerful, soul-winning tool that will help you accomplish the will of the Father for your life on earth.

Helping to fulfill the Great Commission each year until our Lord returns,

—DR. BILL BRIGHT, FOUNDER/CHAIRMAN
CAMPUS CRUSADE FOR CHRIST
COFOUNDER OF THE
GLOBAL PASTORS NETWORK

AUTHOR'S NOTE: Dr. Bill Bright graciously prepared this foreword for the book prior to his death in 2003.

Introduction

THE TESTIMONY OF Sujo John has now gone around the world. A Christian brother from Calcutta, India, Sujo was on the eighty-first floor of the Twin Towers in Manhattan, New York, when the first plane hijacked by Al-Qaeda terrorists struck his building just above the floor on which he was working. Along with thousands of other desperate people, Sujo struggled to make his way out of the burning tower. Just as the building began to collapse, he found himself with fifteen or twenty other people huddled in the basement area. As they lay upon each other in a heap, he began to cry out to Jesus. The others joined him, and through their fear, they all began

1

to call on the name of the Lord Jesus.

When the dust finally settled, Sujo could see that although he had somehow survived, all those around him had died in the building's collapse. But in those few moments as the tower was falling, he was able to help several people into eternity by calling upon the only name that can bring salvation. He had just seconds to touch those people's lives—he will have eternity for them to thank him. Since that time hundreds and even thousands have come to Christ through this dramatic testimony of deliverance.[1]

Taking a brief ride on an elevator, sitting on a city bus, dining in a restaurant, waiting in a line, taking the subway, standing at a crosswalk, strolling through the park, walking down a hallway at the office, hanging out at the pool, attending a soccer game, shopping in the mall, waiting at the checkout counter, cheering at the ballgame, or even receiving a wrong number on the telephone—these events happen to us all, and although we may fail to recognize them as such, they are once-in-a-lifetime opportunities to affect someone for eternity. All in the few seconds when two lives cross paths!

In our lifetimes, most of us will randomly cross

the paths of literally hundreds of thousands of people. We will probably never see these people again this side of eternity—and we are only given a few seconds to touch their souls. If in those few seconds we could make an impact and influence them for Christ, we might indirectly affect millions of people during our brief passage through life. We will likely never know the true influence we have had until we stand before the throne one day and hear the report and the commendation of the Lord for our obedience.

Most of us have never premeditated what we should say in these brief encounters that happen to us so frequently. The Bible tells us to be prepared to give an answer to those who ask about the hope that is in us. (See 1 Peter 3:15.) We should be ready to make a statement. People around us wear weird clothes, nose rings, and tattoos in their attempt to make a statement. Why shouldn't we make our simple statements of faith in turn? Other people curse, swear, or tell dirty stories in public places. Why shouldn't we talk about the salvation and blessings we have received from our amazing relationship with the Lord Jesus?

We should be prepared to take advantage of these momentary encounters. We need to be ready! We can make an impact for eternity in those few moments. Our one touch may be the next step that is needed in the process of their faith. Someone once said that it takes, on the average, seven encounters with a believer—seven times of hearing the gospel—before a person is converted. Who knows what number *your* contact might be? What a privilege to be first. What an honor to be last. But whether we are the one who sows the seed, the one who waters it, or the one who reaps the harvest—we all will receive a reward. What a thrill to be involved in the eternal destiny of another human being!

The story is told of a radical unbeliever who wanted to see George Whitefield preach but did not want to listen to his message. He climbed a tree in a field where Whitefield was speaking just to get a glimpse of the famous revivalist. Deliberately putting fingers in both of his ears, he watched the great preacher without listening to a word he said. But then a stubborn fly landed on his nose, and no matter what he did, he could not shake him off. He unplugged his ears long enough to shoo the fly away, and in those brief seconds, Whitefield proclaimed loudly, "*Him who has ears to hear, let him hear!*" The amazing timing of it so intrigued the man that he listened to the rest of Whitefield's sermon and was gloriously saved.

A brief window of time is given to all of us to touch the lives of even those who we think may not be listening, but who may open their ears long enough for us to penetrate their souls and enlighten their eyes—just for that one brief shining moment.

We are all familiar with the now-famous words of astronaut Neil Armstrong who, as he took the first human step on the surface of the moon, declared, "One small step for man, one giant leap for mankind!" But some of us, who stayed up into the wee hours of the morning that summer night in 1969, will also remember the astronaut reading Scripture as he and his fellow moonwalkers watched the first ever earth-rise from the lunar surface: "In the beginning, God created the heavens and the earth."

As the entire nation watched breathlessly, this man of faith read the opening verses of the Book of Genesis to all on earth who would listen. He became the only man to ever read Scripture verses to Planet Earth from the moon! Think what those few seconds meant to so many people, and what a unique and bold witness that was—the man on the moon telling us about the God of the heavens!

When the seven astronauts of the Columbia space shuttle died in February 2003, some of their words were shared with the entire nation during the touching memorial held for them in Houston, Texas. Astronauts Rick Husband and Michael Anderson were both men of devout faith. At his church's memorial service, a video of Mike Anderson was played in which he said that both he and Husband had faced many challenges during their training: "Rick and I both feel that we were put on this mission for a reason, and we have tried to meet all those challenges with prayer."[2]

In an address to the nation on the afternoon of the Columbia tragedy, President George W. Bush spoke these words: "In the skies today we saw destruction and tragedy. Yet farther than we can see there is comfort and hope. In the words of the prophet Isaiah: 'Lift your eyes and look to the heavens. Who created all these? He who brings out the starry hosts one by one and calls them each by name. Because of His great power and mighty strength, not one of them is missing.' The same Creator who names the stars also knows the names of the seven souls we mourn today. The crew of the shuttle Columbia did not return safely to Earth; yet we can pray that all are safely home."[3]

What a dynamic tribute to men who knew the Lord and allowed their faith to be heralded around the world, even through their tragic deaths. Their seed fell into the ground and brought forth much fruit in just those few minutes, as their message was broadcast over the airwaves of the world.

We have all seen the bold fanatics who attend nationally televised ballgames and hold up signs for Jesus or placards with Scripture verses boldly printed on them. Many of us may have heard the brief testimonies of professional athletes or coaches who, when interviewed on national television at the end of a game, give witness to their faith in Jesus Christ. We have read bumper stickers, overheard faith-filled conversations, or watched others pray in public. These may be just moments in time, but they can make an impact for eternity. Only God knows the fruit of such feeble efforts. Don't underestimate those simple acts of public declaration. Souls hang in the balance.

Giving a witness to your faith does not have to be difficult. The methods given in this book are not beyond anyone's ability. They don't take a college education, cost any money, or demand attendance at a training seminar. All it takes is the courage to simply speak up. All it takes is a desire to proclaim the good news. This is Christianity made simple. This is "Witnessing for Dummies." And we can all do it!

Witnessing for Christ is an exciting, exhilarating adventure of faith that will add energy to our daily walk and excitement to our faith. It is what many of us have been looking for—a simple, forthright way to proclaim the good news of Christ. Try it today. Smile and be happy! Be bold. Look for the open door and the split-second opportunity that God will bring your way.

Throughout this book you will find lists of suggested statements and questions that were given in response to an e-mail request that I sent around the world to many of my ministry friends during the time I was writing this book. These simple suggestions have worked effectively for them as they have shared them with people to open up a conversation about God. You may want to adapt some of these suggestions for your own 60-second approach to the people you meet.

I pray that this collection of practical witnessing tips will not offend the "zealous" evangelist or the "serious" student of the Word of God. Many people believe that it is vital to explain the gospel at the intellectual level of those with whom it is being shared. For those readers, this simplified text may seem insufficient. These words, ideas, and suggestions are not meant to take the place of a thorough explanation of the Scriptures, but they are meant to be used in the unique circumstances where literally seconds count. They are useful when a believer may not have the luxury of fully explaining or presenting the gospel, let alone following it up with proper discipleship methodology.

I have written these statements and collected these ideas, primarily because I often find myself at a loss for words or impacting statements that would be suitable. I have often wanted to remember some simple phrase that could help me take advantage of these kinds of momentary opportunities. Perhaps they will be a help to you as well. May the Holy Spirit grant that you reap eternal fruit from the encounters you have every day of your life.

CHAPTER 1

Preparation

AN ATHLETE PRACTICES. A mountain climber gets into shape. A marathon runner covers countless miles before the big race. A politician polishes his speeches. A businessman develops a sound fiscal strategy. An expectant parent decorates the baby's nursery. A lawyer organizes a brief. And a witness of Jesus Christ prepares a clear and straightforward testimony.

I was once a witness in a court of law. In this particular case, I was not only asked questions by the prosecuting attorney, as a witness *against* the defendant, but I was also cross-examined by the defense attorney. When I inadvertently made a statement about something I said that I had heard someone else say, an objection was raised immediately. It was declared to be hearsay, and my statement was stricken from the record. I had to rephrase my testimony to state only what I myself had personally seen, heard, or experienced. The court, the judge, and especially the defendant's legal team only wanted to hear my version of events. I could not share the words or experiences of others.

We are asked to be a "witness" of the resurrection of Jesus Christ. Being a witness is not *something we do*—it is *someone we are*! The New Testament does not tell us to "go witness." Jesus commands us to "be witnesses" (Acts 1:8). For the early church disciples and apostles, this was a simple task. They merely told of all that they had "seen and heard." (See Acts 4:20; 1 John 1:1.) So it is with us. We are to share our experiences, our observations, and our personal encounters with the risen Lord. To do so, we must be prepared to be succinct and to the point.

I was sharing the distinctiveness of the message of Christ with a friend recently, and I told him there was a major difference between Christianity and other world religions. The reason the Christian faith is so dramatically different from other religions is that all others are philosophies of life based on principles, while Christianity is founded on a Person. Ours is not just a religion—it is a relationship! While believers certainly hold to many life-giving principles, a true Christian is one who has encountered the Person of Jesus Christ and has been changed. We have experienced a living Person through the Holy Spirit. False religions are philosophies that were espoused by dead people. But *our* God is alive! And when you meet the Author, you believe the Book. When you actually meet the Person who calls Himself the "Way, the Truth, and the Life," and tells you that "no one comes to the Father but through Me," you believe Him! This Person—and this relationship—sets Christianity apart from any other "faith" or falsely called "alternative pathways to God."

Some of us have been told that it is offensive to "preach" to people, that it is rude to share the message of Christ. Some people believe we should just live our lives, be examples, and love people unconditionally while we meet some tangible need they may have. They think the church should only be a witness in their social and humanitarian programs. I have even heard people quote statements about preaching the gospel who believe that, *if necessary*, we should use words. But of course, that is not biblical, nor did our Lord tell us to do that. Jesus commanded us to go forth and "preach," proclaiming and telling forth the good news. It is through the foolishness of the message when it is preached, proclaimed, or declared that God saves those who believe.

We must use words, not just our lives, and we should not shrink back from the telling of our message. While it is very important for all of us as believers to live exemplary lives and let our lights shine before men by our good works (Matt. 5:16), we still need to deliver a distinct word. It is not enough to merely influence people "in a positive way." Even unbelievers can do that while doing good to their fellow man. But our calling is different. We are commissioned not only to go, not only to love people and feed the hungry, but also to also preach the gospel and make disciples for Jesus Christ. What a shame it would be to feed people, clothe people, and even bless people, but then allow them to go to hell by failing to introduce them to Christ. The two—doing good and preaching the gospel—are not exclusive. We should do both.

Often what is found to be objectionable is not the sharing of the gospel but the manner or spirit in which it is shared. I do not believe any believer should share words in such a way so as to condemn the sinner or judge the unbeliever. Jesus did not do that. He loved sinners and was even called their friend. Our call is also to proclaim the message of the good news in a loving manner to people who need both kindness and truth. It is the goodness of God that leads people to repentance (Rom. 2:4), and it is the truth that sets them free (John 8:32). This wonderful love of God is what obliges us to proclaim the gospel to others everywhere we go.

> For the love of Christ compels us, because we judge thus: that if One died for all, then all died; and He died for all, that those who live should live no longer for themselves, but for Him who died for them and rose again.
> —2 CORINTHIANS 5:14–15

We understand that faith works through love (Gal. 5:6). I have often preached to my congregation here in Seattle that "people will believe because they are loved." It is the love of God that draws people to Christ. The matchless love of God is what changed our own lives, and it is still working to change the lives of others.

But God demonstrates His own love toward us, in that while we were still sinners, Christ died for us.

—Romans 5:8

In this is love, not that we loved God, but that He loved us and sent His Son to be the propitiation for our sins. Beloved, if God so loved us, we also ought to love one another.

—1 John 4:10–11

And walk in love, as Christ also has loved us and given Himself for us, an offering and a sacrifice to God for a sweet-smelling aroma.

—Ephesians 5:2

But God, who is rich in mercy, because of His great love with which He loved us, even when we were dead in trespasses, made us alive together with Christ (by grace you have been saved).

—Ephesians 2:4–5

For God so loved the world that He gave His only begotten Son, that whoever believes in Him should not perish but have everlasting life. For God did not send His Son into the

world to condemn the world, but that the
world through Him might be saved.
—JOHN 3:16–17

If we will live a life of love as the Bible teaches us (Eph. 5:2), then we will be prepared to express that love toward everyone we meet. As Jesus was moved with compassion for the multitudes of lost people (Matt. 9:36), so we will be moved by that same compassion. This divine love that is poured into our hearts through the Holy Spirit (Rom. 5:5) is the motivation and inspiration we need to do good to all men, to do everything possible to witness to the lost. One of the greatest ways in which we can prepare to share the good news is to allow God's love to abide in our hearts and then be ready to faithfully express that love to everyone we meet.

Preparation also involves spending time in the presence of God, the One who *is* love. Prayer, worship, and meditation on the Word of God will prepare our hearts for daily divine encounters with the people who cross our paths. Not only do we need to know the Book, but we also need to know the Author! The Lord who commissioned us to "go and make disciples" will be faithful to lead people into our path every day.

Here are some tips on making preparations to share the gospel.

1. We should know the Word of God, especially the essential scriptures about the gospel (2 Tim. 2:15).

2. We must stay filled with the Holy Spirit. He is our Helper and the power we need to be an effective witness (Acts 1:8).

3. We ought to stay "prayed up," daily asking the Lord to lead us to people who need Jesus (Acts 4:31; 1 Tim. 2:1–4).

4. We should not get caught up in temporal things but stay ready to witness to people about eternal matters (Ps. 51:12–13; Mark 4:19).

5. We should be ready to give a defense of our faith and declare the lordship of Jesus in our lives (1 Pet. 3:15).

6. We should be active in our local churches so discipleship can be systematically and successfully achieved (Matt. 28:19–20; Heb. 10:25).

CHAPTER 2

What the Bible Says

THE BIBLE SPEAKS for itself. It declares the truth, and it is that truth that will set people free. The Bible tells us that God the Father loved the world so much that He sent His only Son to die for our sins. Jesus Christ, the Son of God, came to seek and to save the lost. He died on the cross for our sins and was raised from the dead on the third day. All who believe in Him are saved from their sins and born again.

Jesus commissioned His followers to go, preach this good news, and make disciples of people from all nationalities. The Holy Spirit empowers us to be witnesses in Jerusalem (our own cities) and also to the ends of the earth.

THE GREAT COMMISSION

In all four Gospels and in the Book of Acts, the commissioning of the disciples is given in the words of the Lord Jesus Himself. This is our primary purpose for living—to fulfill the Great Commission of Christ in our generation.

> Jesus came and spoke to them, saying, "All authority has been given to Me in heaven and on earth. *Go therefore and make disciples* of all the nations, baptizing them in the name of the Father and of the Son and of the Holy Spirit, teaching them to observe all things that I have commanded you; and lo, I am with you always, even to the end of the age." Amen.
>
> —MATTHEW 28:18–20

> And He said to them, "*Go into all the world and preach the gospel* to every creature. He who believes and is baptized will be saved...." And they went out and preached everywhere, the Lord working with them and confirming the word through the accompanying signs. Amen.
>
> —MARK 16:15–16, 20

Then He said to them, "Thus it is written, and thus it was necessary for the Christ to suffer and to rise from the dead the third day, and that *repentance and remission of sins should be preached in His name to all nations*, beginning at Jerusalem. And you are witnesses of these things. Behold, I send the Promise of My Father upon you; but tarry in the city of Jerusalem until you are endued with power from on high."

—LUKE 24:46–49

When He had said this, He showed them His hands and His side. Then the disciples were glad when they saw the Lord. So Jesus said to them again, "Peace to you! *As the Father has sent Me, I also send you*." And when He had said this, He breathed on them, and said to them, "Receive the Holy Spirit. If you forgive the sins of any, they are forgiven them; if you retain the sins of any, they are retained."

—JOHN 20:20–23

"But you shall receive power when the Holy Spirit has come upon you; and *you shall be witnesses to Me* in Jerusalem, and

21

in all Judea and Samaria, and to the end
of the earth."

—ACTS 1:8

THE POWER OF THE GOSPEL

The gospel itself has an inherent power to bring
salvation to the human heart. If we will simply proclaim the good news of what God has
done, it will supernaturally work in the hearts
of those who hear and sincerely desire to know
the truth.

> So, as much as is in me, *I am ready to preach
> the gospel* to you who are in Rome also. For
> I am not ashamed of the gospel of Christ,
> for *it is the power of God* to salvation for
> everyone who believes, for the Jew first and
> also for the Greek.
>
> —ROMANS 1:15–16

> And *this gospel of the kingdom will be preached
> in all the world as a witness* to all the nations,
> and then the end will come.
>
> —MATTHEW 24:14

> But none of these things move me; nor do I
> count my life dear to myself, so that I may

finish my race with joy, and the ministry which I received from the Lord Jesus, *to testify to the gospel* of the grace of God.

—ACTS 20:24

For "whoever calls on the name of the LORD shall be saved." How then shall they call on Him in whom they have not believed? And how shall they believe in Him of whom they have not heard? And how shall they hear without a preacher? And how shall they preach unless they are sent? As it is written: "How beautiful are the feet of those who *preach the gospel of peace*, who bring glad tidings of good things!" But *they have not all obeyed the gospel*. For Isaiah says, "Lord, who has believed our report?" So then faith comes by hearing, and hearing by the word of God.

—ROMANS 10:13–17

For the *message of the cross* is foolishness to those who are perishing, but to us who are being saved it is the power of God.

—1 CORINTHIANS 1:18

Woe is me if I do not *preach the gospel*!

—1 CORINTHIANS 9:16

But even if *our gospel is veiled*, it is veiled to those who are perishing, whose minds the god of this age has blinded, who do not believe, lest the light of the gospel of the glory of Christ, who is the image of God, should shine on them. For we do not preach ourselves, but Christ Jesus the Lord, and ourselves your bondservants for Jesus' sake.
—2 CORINTHIANS 4:3–5

Only let your conduct be *worthy of the gospel of Christ*, so that whether I come and see you or am absent, I may hear of your affairs, that you stand fast in one spirit, with one mind *striving together for the faith of the gospel*, and not in any way terrified by your adversaries, which is to them a proof of perdition, but to you of salvation, and that from God.

—PHILIPPIANS 1:27–28

Therefore do not be ashamed of the testimony of our Lord, nor of me His prisoner, but share with me in the *sufferings for the gospel* according to the power of God, who has saved us and called us with a holy calling, not according to our works, but according to His own purpose and grace which was given to us in Christ Jesus before time began, but has now been revealed by the appearing of our Savior Jesus Christ, who has abolished death and *brought life and immortality to light through the gospel*, to which I was appointed a preacher, an apostle, and a teacher of the Gentiles.

—2 TIMOTHY 1:8–11

WITNESS

The Lord wants us to be bold and clear witnesses of what we have experienced. We have been called by God and anointed by the Holy Spirit to declare what He has done for us and to show who He is to the nations. We are to boldly tell everyone we meet what we have seen and heard about Him.

But Peter and John answered and said to them, "Whether it is right in the sight of God to listen to you more than to God, you judge. For we cannot but *speak the things which we have seen and heard*."

—ACTS 4:19–20

But you shall receive power when the Holy Spirit has come upon you; and *you shall be witnesses* to Me in Jerusalem, and in all Judea and Samaria, and to the end of the earth.

—ACTS 1:8

Then He said to them, "Thus it is written, and thus it was necessary for the Christ to suffer and to rise from the dead the third day, and that repentance and remission of sins should be preached in His name to all nations, beginning at Jerusalem. And *you are witnesses of these things.*"

—LUKE 24:46–48

Therefore they stayed there a long time, speaking boldly in the Lord, who was *bearing witness to the word of His grace*, granting signs and wonders to be done by their hands. And they were preaching the gospel there.

—ACTS 14:3, 7

Now when they had fulfilled all that was written concerning Him, they took Him down from the tree and laid Him in a tomb. But God raised Him from the dead. He was seen for many days by those who came up with Him from Galilee to Jerusalem, *who are His witnesses to the people*. And we declare to you glad tidings—that promise which was made to the fathers.

—ACTS 13:29–32

The word which God sent to the children of Israel, preaching peace through Jesus Christ—He is Lord of all—that word you know, which was proclaimed throughout all Judea, and began from Galilee after the baptism which John preached: how God anointed Jesus of Nazareth with the Holy Spirit and with power, who went about doing good and healing all who were oppressed by the devil, for God was with Him. And *we are witnesses of all things* which He did both in the land of the Jews and in Jerusalem, whom they killed by hanging on a tree. Him God raised up on the third day, and showed Him openly, not to all the people, but *to witnesses chosen* before by God, even to us who ate and drank with Him after He arose from the dead. And *He commanded us to preach to the people, and to testify* that it is He who was ordained by God to be Judge of the living and the dead. *To Him all the prophets witness* that, through His name, whoever believes in Him will receive remission of sins.

—ACTS 10:36–43

But Peter and the other apostles answered and said: "We ought to obey God rather than men. The God of our fathers raised up Jesus whom you murdered by hanging on a tree. Him God has exalted to His right hand to be Prince and Savior, to give repentance to Israel and forgiveness of sins. And *we are His witnesses to these things*, and so also is the Holy Spirit whom God has given to those who obey Him."

—ACTS 5:29–32

And with great power *the apostles gave witness* to the resurrection of the Lord Jesus. And great grace was upon them all.

—ACTS 4:33

CHAPTER 3

Being Led by the Holy Spirit

EVERY BELIEVER WHO wants to be a soulwinner and disciple-maker must learn to listen to the voice, the inner promptings, of the Holy Spirit. He will always be faithful to speak to us and tell us what to do. It is this empowerment of the Holy Spirit and His subsequent guidance that enables us to use the precious seconds we are given to be effective witnesses for the Lord.

There are several benefits that being led by the Holy Spirit brings to our lives and our witness.

The power of the Holy Spirit enables us to be witnesses.

But you shall receive *power when the Holy Spirit* has come upon you; and you shall be witnesses to Me in Jerusalem, and in all Judea and Samaria, and to the end of the earth.

—ACTS 1:8

And when they had prayed, the place where they were assembled together was shaken; and they were all *filled with the Holy Spirit*, and they spoke the word of God with boldness.

—ACTS 4:31

And Ananias went his way and entered the house; and laying his hands on him he said, "Brother Saul, the Lord Jesus, who appeared to you on the road as you came, has sent me that you may receive your sight and *be filled with the Holy Spirit*." Immediately there fell from his eyes something like scales, and he received his sight at once; and he arose and was baptized. So when he had received food, he was strengthened. Then Saul spent some days with the disciples at Damascus.

Immediately he preached the Christ in the synagogues, that He is the Son of God.

—ACTS 9:17–20

God anointed Jesus of Nazareth with *the Holy Spirit and with power*, who went about doing good and healing all who were oppressed by the devil, for God was with Him. And *we are witnesses* of all things.

—ACTS 10:38–39

While Peter was still speaking these words, *the Holy Spirit fell* upon all those who heard the word. And those of the circumcision who believed were astonished, as many as came with Peter, because *the gift of the Holy Spirit* had been poured out on the Gentiles also. For they heard them speak with tongues and magnify God.

—ACTS 10:44–46

Then news of these things came to the ears of the church in Jerusalem, and they sent out Barnabas to go as far as Antioch. When he came and had seen the grace of God, he was glad, and encouraged them all that with purpose of heart they should continue with the Lord. For he was a good man, *full of the Holy Spirit* and of faith. And a great many people were added to the Lord.

—Acts 11:22–24

And when Paul had laid hands on them [the Ephesians], *the Holy Spirit came upon them*, and they spoke with tongues and prophesied.

—Acts 19:6

The Holy Spirit speaks through us as we witness for the Lord.

But when they deliver you up, do not worry about how or what you should speak. For it will be given to you in that hour what you should speak; for it is not you who speak, but *the Spirit of your Father who speaks in you*.

—Matthew 10:19–20

But when the Helper comes, whom I shall send to you from the Father, *the Spirit of truth* who proceeds from the Father, *He will testify of Me*. And *you also will bear witness*.

—John 15:26–27

However, when He, the Spirit of truth, has come, *He will guide you into all truth*; for He will not speak on His own authority, but whatever He hears He will speak; and *He will tell you things to come*. He will glorify Me, for He will take of what is Mine and *declare it to you*.

—JOHN 16:13–14

Jesus answered, "...For this cause I was born, and for this cause I have come into the world, that I should bear witness to the truth. *Everyone who is of the truth hears My voice*."

—JOHN 18:37

The Holy Spirit will guide us—just as He guided the early church disciples.

The deacon Stephen

Then there arose some...disputing with Stephen. And they were not able to resist the wisdom and *the Spirit by which he spoke*.

—ACTS 6:9–10

The evangelist Philip

And behold, a man of Ethiopia...who...had come to Jerusalem to worship, was return-ing. And sitting in his chariot, he was read-ing Isaiah the prophet. Then *the Spirit said* to Philip, "Go near and overtake this chariot."
—ACTS 8:27–29

So he commanded the chariot to stand still. And both Philip and the eunuch went down into the water, and he baptized him. Now when they came up out of the water, *the Spirit of the Lord caught Philip away*, so that the eunuch saw him no more; and he went on his way rejoicing. But Philip was found at Azotus. And passing through, *he preached* in all the cities till he came to Caesarea.
—ACTS 8:38–40

Peter the apostle

While Peter thought about the vision, *the Spirit said to him*, "Behold, three men are seeking you. Arise therefore, *go down and go with them*, doubting nothing; for I have sent them."

—ACTS 10:19–20

34

Then *the Spirit told me to go* with them, doubting nothing. Moreover these six brethren accompanied me, and we entered the man's house.

—Acts 11:12

The prophet Agabus

Then one of them, named Agabus, stood up and *showed by the Spirit* that there was going to be a great famine throughout all the world, which also happened in the days of Claudius Caesar.

—Acts 11:28

And as we stayed many days, a certain prophet named Agabus came down from Judea. When he had come to us, he took Paul's belt, bound his own hands and feet, and said, "*Thus says the Holy Spirit*, 'So shall the Jews at Jerusalem bind the man who owns this belt, and deliver him into the hands of the Gentiles.'"

—Acts 21:10–11

Other first-century prophets

As they ministered to the Lord and fasted, *the Holy Spirit said,* "Now separate to Me Barnabas and Saul for the work to which I have called them." Then, having fasted and prayed, and laid hands on them, they sent them away. So, being *sent out by the Holy Spirit,* they went.

—Acts 13:2–4

James and the church at Jerusalem

For *it seemed good to the Holy Spirit, and to us,* to lay upon you no greater burden than these necessary things.

—Acts 15:28

The apostle Paul

Now when they had gone through Phrygia and the region of Galatia, *they were forbidden by the Holy Spirit to preach the word in Asia.* After they had come to Mysia, they tried to go into Bithynia, but *the Spirit did not permit them.* So passing by Mysia, they came down to Troas. And a vision appeared to Paul in the night. A man of Macedonia stood and pleaded with him, saying, "Come over to Macedonia and help us." Now after he had seen the vision, immediately we sought to go to Macedonia, *concluding that the Lord had called us to preach the gospel to them.*

—ACTS 16:6–10

Now while Paul waited for them at Athens, *his spirit was provoked within him* when he saw that the city was given over to idols. Therefore he reasoned in the synagogue with the Jews and with the Gentile worshipers, and in the marketplace daily with those who happened to be there. Then certain Epicurean and Stoic philosophers encountered him. And some said, "What does this babbler want to say?" Others said, "He seems to be a proclaimer of foreign gods," because he *preached to them Jesus and the resurrection.* And they took him and brought him to the Areopagus, saying, "May we know what this new doctrine is of which you speak? For you are bringing some strange things to our ears. Therefore we want to know what these things mean."

—ACTS 17:16–20

And he reasoned in the synagogue every Sabbath, and persuaded both Jews and Greeks. When Silas and Timothy had come from Macedonia, *Paul was compelled by the Spirit*, and testified to the Jews that Jesus is the Christ.

—ACTS 18:4–5

When these things were accomplished, *Paul purposed in the Spirit*, when he had passed through Macedonia and Achaia, to go to Jerusalem, saying, "After I have been there, I must also see Rome."

—ACTS 19:21

And see, now *I go bound in the spirit* to Jerusalem, not knowing the things that will happen to me there, except that *the Holy Spirit testifies in every city, saying that chains and tribulations await me*. But none of these things move me; nor do I count my life dear to myself, so that I may finish my race with joy, and the ministry which I received from the Lord Jesus, to testify to the gospel of the grace of God.

—ACTS 20:22–24

And finding disciples, we stayed there seven days. *They told Paul through the Spirit* not to go up to Jerusalem.

—ACTS 21:4

The preacher Apollos

Now a certain Jew named Apollos, born at Alexandria, an eloquent man and mighty in the Scriptures, came to Ephesus. This man had been *instructed in the way of the Lord; and being fervent in spirit*, he spoke and taught accurately the things of the Lord, though he knew only the baptism of John. So he began to speak boldly in the synagogue.

—ACTS 18:24–26

The Holy Spirit leads, enables, and assists believers in the fulfillment of their God-given commission.

There is therefore now no condemnation to those who are in Christ Jesus, who do not walk according to the flesh, but *according to the Spirit*.

—ROMANS 8:1

For those who live according to the flesh *set their minds* on the things of the flesh, but

39

those who live according to the Spirit, *the things of the Spirit*.

—ROMANS 8:5

For as many as are *led by the Spirit of God*, these are sons of God. For you did not receive the spirit of bondage again to fear, but you received the Spirit of adoption by whom we cry out, "Abba, Father." *The Spirit Himself bears witness with our spirit* that we are children of God, and if children, then heirs—heirs of God and joint heirs with Christ, if indeed we suffer with Him, that we may also be glorified together.

—ROMANS 8:14–17

Likewise *the Spirit also helps in our weaknesses*. For we do not know what we should pray for as we ought, but *the Spirit Himself makes intercession for us* with groanings which cannot be uttered.

—ROMANS 8:26

These things we also speak, not in words which man's wisdom teaches but which the *Holy Spirit teaches*, comparing spiritual things with spiritual. But the natural man does not receive *the things of the Spirit of*

God, for they are foolishness to him; nor can he know them, because they are spiritually discerned.

—1 CORINTHIANS 2:13–14

But *the manifestation of the Spirit* is given to each one for the profit of all: for to one is given the word of wisdom *through the Spirit*, to another the word of knowledge *through the same Spirit*, to another faith *by the same Spirit*, to another gifts of healings *by the same Spirit*, to another the working of miracles, to another prophecy, to another discerning of spirits, to another different kinds of tongues, to another the interpretation of tongues. But *one and the same Spirit works all these things, distributing to each one* individually as He wills.

—1 CORINTHIANS 12:7–11

For *by one Spirit* we were all baptized into one body—whether Jews or Greeks, whether slaves or free—and *have all been made to drink into one Spirit*.

—1 CORINTHIANS 12:13

You are our epistle written in our hearts, known and read by all men; clearly you are

41

an epistle of Christ, ministered by us, *written not with ink but by the Spirit of the living God*, not on tablets of stone but on tablets of flesh, that is, of the heart.

—2 CORINTHIANS 3:2–3

And since *we have the same spirit of faith*, according to what is written, "I believed and therefore I spoke," we also believe and therefore speak.

—2 CORINTHIANS 4:13

Therefore *He who supplies the Spirit to you and works miracles* among you, does He do it by the works of the law, or by *the hearing of faith*?

—GALATIANS 3:5

I say then: *Walk in the Spirit*, and you shall not fulfill the lust of the flesh.... But if you are *led by the Spirit*, you are not under the law.... If *we live in the Spirit, let us also walk in the Spirit*.

—GALATIANS 5:16, 18, 25

Do not quench the Spirit. Do not despise prophecies. Test all things; hold fast what is good. Abstain from every form of evil.

—1 THESSALONIANS 5:19–22

Now *the Spirit expressly says* that in latter times some will depart from the faith, giving heed to deceiving spirits and doctrines of demons.

—1 TIMOTHY 4:1

Therefore, as *the Holy Spirit says*: "Today, if you will *hear His voice*..."

—HEBREWS 3:7

But *the Holy Spirit also witnesses to us.*

—HEBREWS 10:15

Or do you think that the Scripture says in vain, "*The Spirit who dwells in us yearns jealously*"?

—JAMES 4:5

The prophets have inquired and searched carefully...searching what, or what manner of time, *the Spirit of Christ who was in them was indicating* when He testified beforehand the sufferings of Christ and the glories that would follow. To them it was revealed that, not to themselves, but to us they were ministering the things which now have been reported to you through those who have *preached the gospel to you by the Holy Spirit* sent from heaven—things which angels desire to look into.

—1 PETER 1:10–12

If you are reproached for the name of Christ, blessed are you, *for the Spirit of glory and of God rests upon you.* On their part He is blasphemed, but on your part He is glorified.

—1 PETER 4:14

Prophecy never came by the will of man, but holy men of God spoke as they were *moved by the Holy Spirit.*

—2 PETER 1:21

We are of God. *He who knows God hears us;* he who is not of God does not hear us. By this we *know the spirit of truth* and the spirit of error.

—1 JOHN 4:6

This is He who came by water and blood— Jesus Christ; not only by water, but by water and blood. And it is *the Spirit who bears witness*, because the Spirit is truth.

—1 JOHN 5:6

He who has an ear, *let him hear what the Spirit says to the churches*. To him who overcomes I will give to eat from the tree of life, which is in the midst of the Paradise of God.

—REVELATION 2:7

CHAPTER 4

Redeeming the Time

EVERY ONE OF us has been given a certain allotment of time, and there are opportunities given to us every day that we can use to share Christ with others. No doubt when we pass from this life to the next, we will all realize how much more we could have done to advance the kingdom of God and preach Christ to people who had not yet heard the good news. Perhaps the reason that God will need to wipe tears away from our eyes is that we will be weeping at the thought of lost opportunities for the gospel.

> Walk in wisdom toward those who are outside, *redeeming the time*. Let your speech

always be with grace, seasoned with salt, that you may know how you ought to answer each one.

—COLOSSIANS 4:5–6

Be wise in the way you act toward outsiders; *make the most of every opportunity*. Let your conversation be always full of grace, seasoned with salt, so that you may know how to answer everyone.

—COLOSSIANS 4:5–6, NIV

See then that you walk circumspectly, not as fools but as wise, *redeeming the time*, because the days are evil. Therefore do not be unwise, but understand what the will of the Lord is.

—EPHESIANS 5:15–17

We should each make a fresh commitment to redeem—to buy back—the time and opportunities the Lord gives us. The following list will not only provide you with an idea of the potential opportunities that we all experience in our daily lives, but also the time they might allot for the possibility of sharing the gospel.

How Much Time Do We Really Have?

- In an elevator: fifteen to sixty seconds (Making a gospel statement beats staring at the door!)

- The drive-through of a fast-food restaurant: thirty to sixty seconds

- In a public restroom: thirty to sixty seconds (Be sure to use discretion!)

- At Starbucks: two to five minutes (Share a double gospel—nonfat.)

- Waiting in line: one to five minutes (Hopefully the wait isn't longer than that!)

- While out shopping: two to three minutes per person (Women usually find this method easier than men.)

- In the grocery line: three to four minutes (You can witness to the person in front of you, the person behind you, the clerk who is serving you, and the grocery bagger helping you.)

- On the bus: five to fifteen minutes

FROM ZERO TO ETERNITY IN 60 SECONDS FLAT

- Waiting for baggage at the airport: five to fifteen minutes

- On the tram or subway: five to thirty minutes (Let your light shine—even in the dark.)

- At a seminar: two to three hours (Your spiritual conversation might be better than the seminar itself!)

- At a baseball game: nine innings (seven innings before people start leaving—five innings for Little League)

- At a basketball game: three and one-half quarters (before fans of the losing team start leaving)

- At a football game: two out of four quarters (before fans become too intoxicated)

- At a soccer match: two halves (of running back and forth)

- At a hockey match: three very cold periods (and several body slams)

- At the rodeo: twenty bulls, thirty calves, twenty-five horses, lots of clowns, and some cotton candy

50

- During a fireworks display: thirty minutes (of looking skyward)

- While sunbathing on the beach: one to two hours (Use the right sunscreen, and share with someone of the same gender.)

- At the movies: one hour and fifty-five minutes, on average (but only on the way in, the way out, or during the advertising before the movie starts)

- During an airplane flight: two to five hours domestic; five to twelve hours international

- Classmates: nine months of the school year

- Co-workers: one to five years (average time spent in the same job)

- Neighbors: three to seven years (average time spent living in the same neighborhood)

- Family members: a lifetime

THINGS NOBODY DOES

There are certain things we do mindlessly every day that can actually provide opportunities for sharing the love of Christ with people around us.

In these brief encounters, we can say something that might stay with that person forever.

- Roll down your car window and greet construction workers.

- Go through a drive-through and give the person in the window a tip.

- Instead of cursing the traffic problem and becoming frustrated, irritated, and angry, turn the commute into a time of prayer and intercede for the people in the cars around you.

- Speak to a maid, janitor, or custodian, and thank them for the work they are doing.

- Greet the worker as you pay your fee when exiting a parking garage.

- Talk to people in an elevator.

- Invite the grocery-store clerk to church.

- Pray for a clerk in a store in the mall.

- Thank a police officer who is working at a roadside situation.

- Invite a homeless person to your church, with the promise of helping them with work, clothes, or food if they come. (Be sure you are prepared to do so.)

- Witness to a drive-through teller at the bank.

- Ask a waitress or waiter to join you in prayer over your meal.

- Leave 20 to 25 percent tips for servers to whom you have witnessed.

- Be a witness to the person on the other end of the phone who gets the wrong number.

- When giving directions to a stranger, add the directions to the best local church in the area.

- Say something meaningful while waiting for the Walk sign at an intersection.

- Comment on someone's beautiful baby or child, and weave a gospel greeting into your statement.

- Dress your children up at Halloween and have them hand out invitations to church (in safe neighborhoods).

- Invite neighbor children to your house for an Easter egg hunt.

- Have a summer "Unplugged" concert and barbeque in your backyard.

- Get the neighbors together to sing "God Bless America" on the Fourth of July, and then pray for your country and for peace in the world.

- Set up Christian symbols for a Christmas display in your yard or on your house for the holidays—a star, the wise men, a nativity scene.

- Give Christian gifts as presents—Bibles, music CDs, Christian DVDs.

- Stop alongside the road to offer help to a person in need.

- Offer to pray for people right on the spot when they express a need.

- Take Christmas cards and cookies to your neighbors. Include a clear gospel message in your card and maybe an invitation to your church.

- Use your gifts and talents to bless neighbors or other people around you: change the oil in a car, bake food, give canned foods away, crochet a blanket, draw artwork for a special occasion, clean gutters, paint a fence, blow leaves, mow a lawn, trim a sidewalk, or haul away Christmas trees.

- Give gifts to neighbors on special occasions— birthdays, anniversaries, holidays, graduations, and so on.

- Show a quality kids' video outdoors to neighborhood children in the summer.

- Give someone a ride.

- Stand out in front of your church, and wave to people to come on in (with your pastor's permission).

- Have your toddler sing Bible songs as you shop in the grocery store.

- Randomly make phone calls to numbers from your phone book, and invite people to church. (Be careful to have permission to do this, and use an approved invitation.)

- Walk around your neighborhood while praying, and ask the Lord to lead you to people to minister to or invite to your church.

- Talk about the Lord when you are getting your hair done, your nails manicured, or when having a facial or massage.

- Instead of swearing on the court or field during a sporting competition, try praising God.

- When reading a book in public, in the library, or in the coffee shop, make sure the cover is large and bold and says something that could influence people's faith.

- Always tell people, "God bless you."

- When dialing to get a phone number from an operator, take the opportunity to share Christ with them, pray for them, or encourage them to get back to church. (Make it short and sweet.)

- When standing in a longer line than expected, pray and intercede for the people around you and for the clerk serving you—then thank the clerk when your turn comes.

- Pray and intercede for your neighbors while mowing your lawn or weeding your garden.

INDIRECT STATEMENTS

Sometimes we can influence people indirectly and not have to speak to them directly at all. As we carry on another conversation in their hearing, some of the following statements can introduce life-changing testimonials, and in just a few seconds we can make a difference with a scripture or a thought that might lead someone closer to faith.

Some of these statements include:

- "Wow, if I didn't know better, I would think that the whole world is turning to Christ!"

- "It seems like everyone is going back to church these days."

- "That movie about Christ was amazing. He did all that for us."

- "I heard that the movie *The Passion of the Christ* could possibly become the best-selling movie in history."

- "A lot of people are considering returning to their faith, especially Christianity."

- "I think a lot of people are thinking about spiritual things today."

- "I have heard people talk about Jesus Christ like He was a real Person."

- "Across the world, more people are coming to Jesus Christ today than ever before in history."

- "I heard that Christianity is the fastest-growing religious faith in the entire world."

- "I was reading this scripture the other day…"

- "I was just praying and asking God to make Himself real when…"

- "I've never seen a church like that with so much life and joy."

- "I've never experienced the power of God like that."

- "Did you know that the MVP of that game is a born-again believer?"

- "I think he met the God of the Bible."

- "They got healed through the name of Jesus."

- "God sure is good, isn't He?"

- "I heard that person got healed by the power of God."

- "Miracles still happen today! I heard of one just the other day."

- "Christianity is not a religion—it is a relationship with a very special Person. Jesus Christ is still alive today!"

SUGGESTED STATEMENTS FROM EVANGELISTS

Evangelists of all backgrounds use various statements when trying to make the most of divine encounters, but all have the same objective: to reach the lost for Christ. Dr. Bill Bright said, "If I am in the presence of a person for at least five minutes, I consider it a divine appointment [to share the gospel]." Allow the following statements, collected from evangelists worldwide, "to stir up love and good works" within you (Heb. 10:24).

Who do you think was the greatest person who ever lived? Who has had the most influence on history of any person who has ever lived?

—DR. BILL BRIGHT

Do you have a relationship with God, or are you still searching?

—DR. LUIS PALAU

Are you a Christian yet, or are you still thinking about it?

—WENDELL SMITH

When I prayed this one prayer, it changed my life.

—DR. MARILYN HICKEY

If you died tonight, would you go to heaven?

—ANONYMOUS

Have you ever accepted Jesus as your Savior? Let's do it right now. Take my hand, and let's pray.

—SHARON ALTIG-SMITH

Where is God for you? What does that feel like?

—DIANE DIVET

My ministry is called Heart Cry. Are you satisfied with your life? What's your heart cry?

—RACHEL HICKSON

Let me pray for you. (Then touch them and impart a touch of the Holy Spirit.)

—PHIL PRINGLE

I have a philosophy that everyone was born for a reason. Do you know what you were born for? When you are dying, will you know why you lived? (Then share a word of knowledge about their future as the Holy Spirit might lead.)

—CINDY JACOBS

I am just a nobody, telling everybody that there is a Somebody who can save anybody.

—MELVIN GRAHAM

Wouldn't you like to open your heart and let Jesus in?

—DAVE SOLEIM

> Can you trust God as much as you trust that rope? (Say this to a fellow worker hanging by a rope at a construction site.)
>
> —LEE MORSE

> Are you ready for heaven?
>
> —BILLY JOE DAUGHERTY

> Has anyone ever told you the difference between religion and a relationship with Jesus Christ?[1]
>
> —WILLIAM FAY

CHAPTER 5

The Power of the Name of Jesus Christ

THERE IS BOTH power and offense in the name of Jesus. Some people are offended by the name of Jesus because it is so spiritually commanding. If a person is under the influence of an evil spirit (because they have willingly opened their heart to that spirit through sin), then they will most likely react to your use of the name of Jesus Christ. In many nations today it is not politically correct to mention the name of Jesus, but it is acceptable to use the name of Muhammad or some other false religion's leader. Ironically, it is acceptable to talk about God in general in America, but to mention the name of Jesus Christ can often get you into big trouble. Why? Because there is power in that name!

The reason the name of Jesus has become a swear word or a curse in many people's common language is because the devil would like to take the name that is above every name, bring it down, and cast it underfoot to be trampled. But the Bible says that even the wrath of man will praise Him! (See Psalm 76:10.) You will never hear someone curse by using the name of Buddha or some other false prophet. The devil will always attack the name above all names in an attempt to dishonor it.

The name of Jesus is not just an offense. There is power in that name, and believers should not be afraid of speaking it or using it to bring help and salvation to people. The early church apostles were threatened and told not to speak in that name at all (Acts 5:28). But Peter boldly declared that they would obey God rather than men—they would not cease speaking that name and telling of the things they had seen and heard.

Don't be afraid to use His name! There is salvation in no other name on earth or in heaven (Acts 4:12). Be bold, and the Lord will help and protect you as you proclaim His wonderful name—the name of Jesus Christ, our Lord and Savior (Prov. 18:10).

PHRASES TO USE WITH THE NAME OF JESUS

When witnessing, use these phrases as you incorporate the name of Jesus in your conversation:

- "Praise the name of Jesus!"

- "Jesus is my Lord and Savior."

- "Do you know Jesus?"

- "In the name of Jesus…" (as you pray)

- "O Jesus, help us."

- "The Lord Jesus Christ is the Son of God."

- "Jesus of Nazareth was the greatest person who ever lived!"

- "I give glory (or credit) to my Lord and Savior, Jesus Christ."

- "Jesus Christ is Lord!"

- "Lord Jesus, You are so good."

- "Praise You, Lord Jesus!"

- "Has anyone ever told you what Jesus Christ really did?"

- "What would Jesus do?"

- "I wonder what Jesus would do."

- "Thank You, Jesus!"

CHAPTER 6

Practical Ways to Open a Conversation

SOME BELIEVERS WOULD love to be witnesses for Jesus, but they find it difficult to initiate conversations about the gospel. This chapter contains some practical tips for opening such a conversation.

DIRECT COMMENTS

The name of Jesus is a powerful witnessing tool, but as you prepare to share the gospel in a short amount of time with someone, sometimes a more direct approach is best.

We can often simply make a short, straightforward statement to people and trust God to influence them for the kingdom of God. God will honor His Word, and as the name of Jesus is lifted up, He will draw people unto Himself.

Here are some direct comments:

- "I like you—you should go to my church!"

- "You look like you would make a good believer."

- "You should be a Christian!"

- "You're not far from the kingdom of God."

- "The Lord was sure good to you to give you such a beautiful family (or baby, house, or car)!"

- "What a wonderful Creator God is!"

- "Isn't God good?"

- "God was showing off when He made this place!"

- "We may never meet again, so I want you to have this." (Then share the gospel as if it were a gift.)

- "May I give you a gift? God bless you."

- "I'd like you to have this."

Direct comments that work

> I'm a Christian, and if God can change my life the way He has, I know that He can help you with your problem.
>
> —Leon Sandberg

> You know, there's more to this life than you think.
>
> —Rick Greene

> When talking with other moms about their kids and what they will grow up to be, I sometimes say: "When you think about your children's future, do you ever help them plan to go to heaven?"
>
> —Jennifer Kraker

QUESTIONS

Another way of introducing the gospel into a conversation is through a direct question. Asking a question can be a very effective way to open a conversation. It usually demands a response of some kind, and most people will cooperate and give an answer.

Here are some examples of great conversation-starting questions:

- "Who do you believe was the greatest person in history?"

- "Who do you think has made the single greatest impact on people's lives and in the world?"

- "If you died tonight, are you sure you would go to heaven? Why? Why not?"

- "I am praying for people today. Is there anything I can pray about for you?"

- "Is this your first trip to _____? Don't miss the church at _____!"

- "Do you know of any good churches around here?"

- "What do you think when you hear people talking about God?"

- "When was the last time you went to church?"

- "If you could ask God for one miracle in your life, what would you ask Him for?"

- "What is the greatest need in your life, and how do you plan to meet it?"

Practical Ways to Open a Conversation

- "Where do you think you will spend eternity?"

- "Who is the most important person in your life and why?"

- "How would you define absolute truth?"

- "What words would you use to describe God? What words would you use to describe man?"

- "What has kept you from believing in God?"

- "What has kept you from attending a church?"

- "I believe the Lord wants me to tell you..."

- "God wants you to know..."

- "What do you think God thinks about that?"

- "Have you ever had a prayer answered by God?"

- "Who do you call on when you are in danger?"

- "Can you suggest a good church that I can go to in this area?"

- "Jesus changed my life. Who changed yours?"

- "I noticed you have a crucifix (or a cross or some other religious statue or object). What personal significance does that have for you? Why do you have that in your car (on your bumper or shirt)?"

- "I noticed you did something to help you have good luck. Would you be nice enough to tell me why you believe that way?"

- "Do you believe there is life after death?"

- "What kind of person will continue living with God? Do you think that you are one of those kinds of people? Why?"

- "Do you think heaven really exists?"

Questions from real people that really work

> If you could be 100 percent sure that God is real and that He wants a personal, intimate relationship with you, would you want to know Him?
>
> —AMY BENTHIN

> Why do you think there are so many problems facing us in the world today?
>
> —MARC ESTES

Do you believe you will go to heaven when you die? Why? Why not?
—FRANCIS ANFUSO

So where do you go to church?
—PAUL FRIEDERICI

Do you believe in hell? What type of person will go there? Do you need prayer? What's going on in your life?
—JOEL PIKE

God knows where you are, God knows where you need to be, and only God knows how to get you there.
—ART SEPULVEDA

You might think this is strange, but God just spoke to me about you. He wants you to know that He loves you.
—ERIK TAMMARU

Do you have any idea where I can find God?
—ANDREW PRAKASAM

What do you think about Jesus?
—GREG BUCKIEWICZ

In the South (the "Bible Belt") I sometimes ask people about their faith. If they say, "Oh, I'm a Baptist," I then say, "There are two kinds of Baptists. Those who are going to hell and those who are going to heaven. Which one are you?" (This can be used with any denomination.) If they say, "I'm going to heaven," I then respond, "Why would He let you in?"

—RICK SNOW

Say I believe in God and you don't. If there is *no* God, we both lose when we die. But if there *is* a God, you still lose, and I have everything to gain.

—BLAISE PASCAL

TELLING A STORY

Simply reporting a narrative in front of others can be a great way to share your testimony and the truth in a nonthreatening way. Refer to current events or something that has happened in your personal life. These words can be spoken directly to another person or indirectly by speaking to a friend while you know others are listening.

- "We had friends who died on Flight 261."

- "I knew a young man who was on an airplane that hit the Twin Towers in New York on September 11."

- "I heard recently that Christian churches are booming."

- "They talked about Jesus Christ as if He was a real Person."

- "That disaster sure caused a lot of people to pray."

- "Did you hear about how God saved that person?"

- "I heard that movie about the Christ set all kinds of records."

- "The person I knew who had the greatest faith was..."

- "I heard a story about..."

NEGATIVE COMMENTS

When bad things happen, and especially when they happen to "good" people, we should be prepared to give an answer to people's questions and confusion. Here are some helpful phrases that can be used in the face of negative comments to speak up and defend the reputation of the Lord Jesus Christ and the truth of God's Word.

- "Those were not acts of God. They were acts of Satan, the god of this world."

- "Those things are the result of sin in the hearts of wicked people."

- "The Bible says that everything that can be shaken will be shaken."

- "Jesus would never do that to anybody."

- "God doesn't hate the world. God loves the world. He loves people. We know that because He sent His Son to die for us."

- "Just like God allows you and me to choose our way of life, He also allows wicked men to choose evil."

- "True Bible-believing Christians love people. We don't hate them."

- "No, that is not true. The Bible says…"

- "No, Jesus did not say that. He actually said..."

- "Jesus certainly would not condone war, but He did predict that it would happen."

- "It is hatred and sin in people's hearts that causes things like war and terrorism."

- "Jesus never condoned the murder of innocent people. Other religions apparently do, but Jesus of Nazareth never did."

- "Sometimes people are ignorant of the Bible and what it really says about God, and therefore they misquote it."

- "Many people misquote Jesus. Have you ever actually read what He said or taught?"

- "The God I know is not the god you are talking about."

- "If you knew the Lord Jesus like I do, I don't think you would say that."

- "God is a good God. He is so good that He sent His Son, Jesus, to die for our sins."

- "There will always be evil in the world. But God is so good, He can turn evil around for good in the lives of those who will call upon Him and put their trust in Him."

CHAPTER 7

When You Can Take Some Time

As I BOARDED a long-distance flight from Seattle to Asia and found my seat in the business class, I was hoping to have an empty seat next to me so that I could have time to rest, relax, and do some reading. I did not particularly want to engage in a conversation on this particular flight. But then a man sat down next to me, and as the plane took off, so did our dialogue. This was obviously one of those times when I had more than just a few moments to share the gospel, and it was also apparent that this was a divine opportunity, planned by the Lord in order to help this man.

Within an hour or so, the discussion took a turn into issues of faith, and I learned that the man was a true seeker. Finally I was able to ask him if anyone had ever actually shared with him what Jesus had done and how to become a Christian. He indicated that no one had shared with him. What a wonderful time I had sharing the greatest story ever told with this hungry man. We were even able to pray together before our flight was over.

The Lord will sometimes give us open doors such as this to share the gospel more fully with those we encounter in our daily lives. We need to be prepared to go through that open doorway into another person's heart when the invitation is obvious. Here are some "door openers" for those types of occasions.

- "Has anyone ever explained to you how to become a Christian?"

- "Has anyone ever told you the story of what Jesus Christ actually did?"

- "Did you see the movie *The Passion of the Christ*? Do you understand what Jesus did?"

- "What caused you to become an atheist?"

- "What has kept you from believing?"

- "May I pray for you?"

- "Oh, I love Muslims, and Muslims love me!"

- "Do you believe in God? That's great! But how has believing in God changed your life?"

- "Have you ever asked yourself why you were created?"

- "Did you know that God has a plan for your life that is specific and unique to you as an individual?"

"Door openers" from real people that really work

> Years ago I prayed one prayer that changed my life.
> —DR. MARILYN HICKEY

> We are always here for you because God loves you.
> —DAVID PACKIAM

> "Tell me about your life—how you grew up, your family." Later ask, "What do you

base your life on? Do you have any key beliefs or relationships?"

—JEFF KEMP

Are you ready for heaven?
—BILLY JOE DAUGHERTY

When I asked Jesus to be the Lord of my life, He totally changed my future. I want to pray with you to receive Him.

—MARTY MACDONALD

Your biggest obstacle to Christianity seems to be Christians. Just remember, they're not God, and you don't have to be like them.

—REECE BOWLING

Who is Jesus to you?
—JAMES MONAGHAN

"What is your name?" After they have told me their name, I purposely call them someone else's name later in the conversation. When I ask, "That is your name, right?" they usually reply with their correct name. Then I say, "You see, God has a correct name, too!"

—TEDD CRAVEN

Healing is temporal, but heaven is trans-
formational.

—TONY ALWARD

May I tell you a story that changed my life?

—JON OLETZKE

To Catholics: Do you know what the
Blessed Virgin Mary said? "Whatsoever
He [Jesus] says, do it" (John 2:5). And Jesus
said, "Except a man be born again he can-
not enter the kingdom of God" (John 3:3).
Have you been born again?

—BILL BROWN

"Do you want to be freed from Satan's
power?" Of course, someone from an
African culture would not view this question as being odd. Most persons bound by
Satan and his demons want to be freed. I
am sure that many persons even in America
need to be liberated from bondage.

—DOUG PERKINS

Life is a challenge! Who do you turn to
when you are up against a wall?

—DR. PRINCE GUNERATNAM

When a person describes a bad situation, such as an illness, I say to them: "I believe that God answers prayer. May I pray with you about this? We have a group at our church that will also pray for you."

—EARNEST GENTILE

Do you ever think about spiritual things?

—JARED HUGHES

I'm looking for several people who are interested in learning more about God.

—RON YOHE

"Hi there, _____ (looking at a waiter who is wearing a nametag). You need to ask me why I am smiling so much." The person always responds, "Why are you smiling?"

—LOUIS DEMEO

Are you looking for a God whose presence lives inside of you and will never leave you, filling all the voids in your life?

—WIL LAKE

I remember, as a child, hearing my pastor, Reg Layzell, challenge an atheist to say just one prayer and see what would happen.

This is the prayer they were to pray: "Jesus, save my soul, if I have a soul."

—HOWARD RACHINSKI

I need to ask your forgiveness. I have not told you about the most important thing in my life. I have not shared how you can have a personal relationship with Jesus Christ, and I want you to know I'm sorry.[2]

—WILLIAM FAY

A Jewish friend of mine to whom I have been witnessing for years said, "Rick, when I decide to accept Jesus, I will go through you."

—RICK ALTIG

Dr. Bill Bright would often encourage seekers to try the "thirty-day challenge"—reading one chapter of the Gospel of John every day, beginning with prayer asking God to reveal the reality of His Son, Jesus, to them as they read. Most people never made it through the month before they encountered the living reality of Christ.

Chapter 8

Gospel Conversations

There are many ways to introduce the gospel into conversations. Here are just a few that might work for you.

Current Events

The headlines of today's newspapers can provide a great opportunity to weave the divine perspective on life into virtually any conversation. Any news item can be an open door for the truth to be shared. The bad news that the media report can be turned into the good news by a wise soulwinner. For example:

- "I thought the words of some of those astronauts that were shared at their memorial service were very touching, especially the Scripture passages they quoted."

- "I understand that many of the people who experienced the horror of September 11 called on the name of the Lord. It was certainly a day to put your faith in God."

- "Everyone believes in God in times like these."

- "Prayer is a powerful thing."

- "I believe there is a God who answers prayer!"

- "War is a terrible thing. We should pray that lives will be spared and that this will end quickly."

- "I believe the Lord will help our military personnel in their time of trial."

- "Our president sure needs our prayers."

- "If ever we needed to pray for our politicians, it's now."

- "What a tragedy! We need to pray for those people."

- "All over the world, there are horrible events taking place. The Bible predicted these things would happen."

- "Jesus Christ prophesied that events like these would take place."

- "The Bible actually predicts events like these."

- "Would you mind if I led us in a prayer for those people?"

- "Only the Scriptures can explain why people do those kind of things."

- "Sin is a horrible thing in the human heart. Look what destructive things can happen when a person gives themselves over to evil."

- "The Bible says that 'one sinner destroys much good.'"

Real solutions from real people

> If you'd like to tell me your husband's name, then my husband and I will pray tonight for him to be healed.
>
> —PAM BROWN

What do you think will happen to bin Laden after he dies?

—JAMES MONAGHAN

WHEN YOU DON'T FEEL FRIENDLY OR TALKATIVE

We certainly don't make our decisions—especially life-changing ones—on our feelings or physical condition, but the reality is that there may be times when you may not have the energy to fully share Christ with a person. In some cases, there may be other ways to influence them in a godly way.

- Smile
- "God bless you."
- "The Lord bless you."
- "Jesus loves you."
- "The Lord is good."
- "Praise God!"
- "Well, praise the Lord!"
- "Here is something you might find interesting to read."
- "Here's my card."
- "I will pray for you."
- "Let me send you something."
- "Hallelujah!"

90

- "The good Lord must love you."
- "Ain't God good?"

GREAT SCRIPTURES TO SHARE

The following list contains some of the choice Scripture verses in the entire Bible that are excellent for sharing the gospel with unsaved people.

> For God so loved the world that He gave His only begotten Son, that whoever believes in Him should not perish but have everlasting life. For God did not send His Son into the world to condemn the world, but that the world through Him might be saved.
> —JOHN 3:16–17

> And truly Jesus did many other signs in the presence of His disciples, which are not written in this book; but these are written that you may believe that Jesus is the Christ, the Son of God, and that believing you may have life in His name.
> —JOHN 20:30–31

> And this is the testimony: that God has given us eternal life, and this life is in His Son. He who has the Son has life; he who

does not have the Son of God does not have life.

—1 JOHN 5:11–12

He was in the world, and the world was made through Him, and the world did not know Him. He came to His own, and His own did not receive Him. But as many as received Him, to them He gave the right to become children of God, to those who believe in His name.

—JOHN 1:10–12

The Lord is not slack concerning His promise, as some count slackness, but is longsuffering toward us, not willing that any should perish but that all should come to repentance.

—2 PETER 3:9

For this is good and acceptable in the sight of God our Savior, who desires all men to be saved and to come to the knowledge of the truth.

—1 TIMOTHY 2:3–4

And he brought them out and said, "Sirs, what must I do to be saved?" So they said,

"Believe on the Lord Jesus Christ, and you
will be saved, you and your household."

—Acts 16:30–31

So Philip ran to him, and heard him reading the prophet Isaiah, and said, "Do you
understand what you are reading?" And he
said, "How can I, unless someone guides
me?" And he asked Philip to come up and
sit with him. The place in the Scripture
which he read was this: "He was led as a
sheep to the slaughter; and as a lamb before
its shearer is silent, so He opened not His
mouth. In His humiliation His justice
was taken away, and who will declare His
generation? For His life is taken from the
earth." So the eunuch answered Philip and
said, "I ask you, of whom does the prophet
say this, of himself or of some other man?"
Then Philip opened his mouth, and beginning at this Scripture, preached Jesus to
him. Now as they went down the road,
they came to some water. And the eunuch
said, "See, here is water. What hinders me
from being baptized?" Then Philip said,
"If you believe with all your heart, you
may." And he answered and said, "I believe
that Jesus Christ is the Son of God." So he

commanded the chariot to stand still. And both Philip and the eunuch went down into the water, and he baptized him.

—ACTS 8:30–38

PRAYERS

I am amazed how many people will respond if you offer to pray for them and how many people will respect you when you pray in public. I once boarded an airplane, a large 747 jet that was headed overseas. I felt the Holy Spirit prompt me to go to the cockpit and pray for the pilots. At the appropriate time—before takeoff and while people were still boarding the plane—I walked to the open cockpit door and asked the pilots if I could pray for them. After they gave their permission, I prayed for their alertness and skill and for God's protection on our flight. I thanked them, and then I told them I was a pastor and if they needed my services to feel free to call on me. It was a smooth and enjoyable trip, and they thanked me before I got off the flight. While things have certainly changed since September 11, and you may not physically be allowed into the cockpit for security reasons, you can certainly pray for your pilots from your seat and send a message to the pilots through your flight attendant.

Another time I was led by the Spirit to intercede on a flight from South America back to Miami, Florida. In this particular case, I felt the Lord tell me to kneel down and pray at my seat. My seat happened to be adjacent to the galley area, but although there were many people coming and going, I knew the Lord wanted me to pray in that manner. At first I struggled with obeying the Lord in that kind of obvious public display, but I eventually yielded to the Lord's nudging and knelt there for over an hour praying. I am sure some people must have thought it was a new and creative way to sleep on an airplane!

Later in the flight, a message came to me at my seat from the captain, saying that the tower in Miami had relayed word of an emergency in our home church and that I was to call there immediately upon landing. I had never received a message like that before; in fact, I had never heard of anyone receiving word of an emergency through the pilots of a large commercial airliner such as we were on. But the Lord had surely been preparing me for the urgency of the situation by prompting me to pray.

Other more simple experiences of praying in

public in order to introduce the gospel include praying over a meal either on an airline or in a restaurant, and even asking the person next to you to join you in prayer. People usually oblige and will even respect you for doing it. This kind of bold but simple witness can open doors for you to speak to someone about their own need or even pray for them before that encounter is over.

Here are some examples of simple prayers and ways to introduce prayer that can impact the people around you:

- "Lord Jesus, bless this food."

- "Lord, we pray You will protect us on this trip."

- "Could I say a prayer for you?"

- "How can I pray for you?"

- "I am praying for people today, and I wonder how I might pray for you."

Other prayer ideas include:

- Praying for a flight attendant personally during a flight

- Praying for the healing of others: "Lord, I pray that You would heal this person. Touch their body and make them whole, in the name of Jesus Christ."

- Prayer for protection: "Lord, I pray that You would protect this person and his family."

- Prayer of blessing over children: "Lord Jesus, I pray a blessing over these children—that their angels would protect them, that they would come to know You at an early age, and that they would have great faith. In Jesus' name I pray."

- Prayer for difficult circumstances: "Lord, I pray that You would turn this situation around for my friend and help them through it. Help them see that You are real and that You love them, despite what is going on in their life."

- The prayer of Jabez: "Lord, I pray that You would bless them and enlarge their territory, and that You would help them come to know You personally through our Lord and Savior, Jesus Christ."

CHAPTER 9

The Supernatural Gifts of the Holy Spirit

THE HOLY SPIRIT gives supernatural enablement to believers in order to bless the people around them. These spiritual gifts are an expression of God's love to the world, given to help Christians in their walk of faith and to bring others to Christ. (See 1 Corinthians 12 and Romans 12.) They can be wonderful divine assets to help us lead people to Christ.

Jesus used spiritual gifts in His ministry. As He was speaking to the woman at the well, He used a word of knowledge and a word of prophecy. With Nathaniel He also used a word of knowledge, and He used the gifts of healing to help countless others. The apostles did the same in their ministry in the first-century church. (To learn of their exploits, I would encourage you to read the entire Book of Acts in one sitting.) The good news is that *we can do the same* as we are sensitive to the voice of the Holy Spirit and seek to bless people, love them, and lead them to faith in Christ.

Here is a list of some of the various gifts of the Spirit and how they may help you to be a witness for Jesus Christ.

- **Gift of mercy**—Allow the Holy Spirit to fill you with compassion for a person, compassion that will move you to be a witness of Christ to them (Matt. 9:38). You might say, "May I help you? The Lord wants you to know how much He loves you and that He knows what you have been going through. God bless you."

- **Word of faith**—Expect the Holy Spirit to give you a word of encouragement or edification for another person (Acts 14:9–10). You might say, "God is going to make Himself real to you! I believe that when you lay your head on your pillow tonight, God will begin to speak to you."

100

- **Word of wisdom**—The Holy Spirit may give you an insight of wisdom as to what a person should do (Acts 9:17). For example, you might say, "I think it would be really good if you were to do this."

- **Word of knowledge**—A word of knowledge is a revelation of private information about a person that helps build their faith (John 4:17–18). You might say, "You have struggled with addiction, haven't you?" Or, "What happened between you and your father?"

- **Gifts of healing**—This is a special anointing to bring physical healing to a person's body through the power of the Holy Spirit and the name of Jesus (Acts 3:6–7). For example, you might say, "Let me pray for you, and I believe the Lord will heal you."

- **Gift of miracles**—Although the gift of miracles is more rare, it can be an amazing witness for Christ. It is a special faith for miraculous divine intervention in a person's life that comes through the leading and power of the Holy Spirit (Acts 8:13). You might say, "I believe the Lord can do miracles. Let me pray for you that the Lord will supernaturally help you."

- **Gift of prophecy**—Prophecy shares a revelation into a person's future, based on Scripture and personal insight given from the Holy Spirit (Acts 21:9). You might say, "I believe the Lord is going to heal your family in a wonderful way, and when He does, be sure to give Him the glory!"

- **Gift of exhortation**—With the gift of exhortation, you have the God-given ability to encourage and inspire people with your words. Use this gift to stimulate people to think seriously about eternal things and the good news of Jesus Christ (Rom. 12:7). You might say, "God is good, and He wants you to know that He loves you. I believe you would make a great believer. Let me tell you a story."

- **Gift of giving**—This is a grace given to share your resources with another person to help meet their needs in a tangible way (Acts 11:29). (However, you should always be cautious about giving money to people. Instead, perhaps, consider giving food or clothing.) You might say, "I believe the Lord wants me to bless you with this small gift so you will know how much He loves you."

Please note: the gifts of the Spirit are subjective, and they must always be judged by the revelation of the Bible—the Word of God. They should not be used flippantly or presumptuously, but rather discreetly and in the fear of the Lord. Any words shared with another person should come only from the prompting of the Holy Spirit and not from our own minds. Ministry on this level is not about "creative" ideas and thoughts, but rather it is about sensitivity to the Holy Spirit and His leading.

CHAPTER 10

Proclaiming the Gospel

WE ARE NOT called to "explain" the gospel but to "proclaim" the gospel! Sometimes we try too hard to convince people of absolute truth, when we might be better advised to simply share the truth and let it work for itself as the Holy Spirit does His work in drawing the lost to Christ.

Let's look at some examples of this principle that can be found in Scripture.

The apostles' doctrinal explanation of the gospel

> And without controversy great is the mystery of godliness: God was manifested in the flesh, justified in the Spirit, seen by angels,

105

preached among the Gentiles, believed on
in the world, received up in glory.

—1 TIMOTHY 3:16

Paul preaches the gospel to the Philippian jailer

And he brought them out and said, "Sirs,
what must I do to be saved?" So they said,
"Believe on the Lord Jesus Christ, and you
will be saved, you and your household."

—ACTS 16:30–31

Peter preaches the gospel to Cornelius and his household

"So I sent to you immediately, and you
have done well to come. Now therefore,
we are all present before God, to hear all
the things commanded you by God." Then
Peter opened his mouth and said: "In truth
I perceive that God shows no partiality.
But in every nation whoever fears Him and
works righteousness is accepted by Him.
The word which God sent to the children
of Israel, preaching peace through Jesus
Christ—He is Lord of all—that word you
know, which was proclaimed throughout
all Judea, and began from Galilee after

the baptism which John preached: how God anointed Jesus of Nazareth with the Holy Spirit and with power, who went about doing good and healing all who were oppressed by the devil, for God was with Him. And we are witnesses of all things which He did both in the land of the Jews and in Jerusalem, whom they killed by hanging on a tree. Him God raised up on the third day, and showed Him openly."

—ACTS 10:33–40

The greatest story ever told

For I delivered to you first of all that which I also received: that Christ died for our sins according to the Scriptures, and that He was buried, and that He rose again the third day according to the Scriptures, and that He was seen by Cephas, then by the twelve.

—1 CORINTHIANS 15:3–5

Peter preaches the first gospel message

"Therefore let all the house of Israel know assuredly that God has made this Jesus, whom you crucified, both Lord and Christ." Now when they heard this, they were cut to the heart, and said to Peter and the rest of

the apostles, "Men and brethren, what shall
we do?" Then Peter said to them, "Repent,
and let every one of you be baptized in the
name of Jesus Christ for the remission of
sins; and you shall receive the gift of the
Holy Spirit."

—ACTS 2:36–38

The "Peter Package"

1. Repent
2. Be baptized
3. Receive the gift of the Holy Spirit (Acts 2:38)

The gospel is simply the good news that God
loves us and has provided a way for us to have
forgiveness of sins and eternal life—by believing
in His Son and accepting Him as our Lord and
Savior. It is to believe that God sent His Son,
Jesus, to die on the cross for our sins, and that
God raised Him from the dead on the third day.

Our task is to go forth and spell it out for
people. Spreading the gospel has these two com-
ponents: we are called to *go*, and we are called to
say something. It is the "go-spel!" If we will go, the
Lord will then help us to "spell it out." What can
we say to people if they ask for more information,

108

if they are interested, if they open their hearts and want help? We can tell them our story *and* His story! No one can argue with those two things.

1. Your story—This is your testimony of what the Lord has done for you.

2. His story—This is the biblical record of what God did when He sent His Son to die for us.

No one can deny what happened to you. They were not there. You were! In the same way, no one can deny the fact that a Person named Jesus Christ actually lived. He is the most compelling figure in all of human history. His story has even divided history in half—the years before His birth and the years since. If this Jesus is who He says He is and who others say He is, then everything changes. A person cannot deny the facts. They must decide what they will do with Jesus Christ.

Our part in this process is simple. We simply relate the story (both ours and His), and then let the gospel do its work in people's hearts! Go and spell it out. The Lord will be with you.

THE POWER OF TRACTS

Sometimes we are able to give a person a book, booklet, or printed tract that contains a presentation of the gospel of some sort that they can read at their leisure. Although a personal witness is always required on our part, the printed page can also be a powerful means of eternal influence in a person's life. Countless numbers of people have been born again by reading a Bible tract or a printed presentation of the good news.

Charles Spurgeon on tracts

> I well remember distributing them in a town in England where tracts had never been distributed before, and going from house to house, and telling in humble language the things of the kingdom of God. I might have done nothing, if I had not been encouraged by finding myself able to do something.... [Tracts are] adapted to those persons who have but little power and little ability, but nevertheless, wish to do something for Christ. They have not the tongue of the eloquent, but they may have the hand of the diligent. They cannot stand and preach, but they can stand

and distribute here and there these silent preachers.... They may buy their thousand tracts, and these they can distribute and broadcast.

I look upon the giving away of a religious tract as only the first step for action not to be compared with many another deed done for Christ; but were it not for the first step we might never reach to the second, but that first attained, we are encouraged to take another, and so at the last...there is a real service of Christ in the distribution of the gospel in its printed form, a service the result of which heaven alone shall disclose, and the judgment day alone discover. How many thousands have been carried to heaven instrumentally upon the wings of these tracts, none can tell.

I might say, if it were right to quote such a Scripture, "The leaves were for the healing of the nations"—verily they are so. Scattered where the whole tree could scarcely be carried, the very leaves have had a medicinal and a healing virtue in them and the real word of truth, the simple statement of a Savior crucified and of a sinner who shall be saved by simply trusting in the Savior, has been greatly blessed, and many thousand souls have been led into the kingdom of heaven by this simple means. Let each one of us, if we have done nothing for Christ, begin to do something now. The distribution of tracts is the first thing.[1]

"Gospel Tracts and How to Use Them" by Pastor Ron Yohe

If Paul meant, "by all means," he no doubt would have used gospel tracts as a means to reach the lost. A Christian book relates the true story of a diver who saw a piece of paper clutched in the shell of an oyster. The man grabbed it, found that it was a gospel tract and said, "I can't hold out any longer. His mercy is so great that He has caused His Word to follow me even to the bottom of the ocean." God used that tract to save that man.

Why should a Christian use tracts? We should use them simply because God uses them. He used a tract to save the great missionary Hudson Taylor, as well as innumerable others. That fact alone should be enough incentive for a Christian to always use tracts to reach the lost, but there are even more reasons why we should use them.

- Tracts can provide an opening for us to share our faith. We can watch people's reaction as we give them a tract, and see if they are open to listening to spiritual things.

- They can do the witnessing for us. If we are too timid to speak to someone about the things of God, we can at least give them a tract, or leave it lying around so that someone will pick it up.

- They speak to the individuals when they are ready—they don't read it until they want to.

- They can find their way into people's homes when we can't.

- They don't get into arguments; they just state their case.

Dr. Oswald J. Smith said, "The only way to carry out the Great Commission will be by the means of the printed page." Charles Spurgeon stated, "When preaching and private talk are not available, you need to have a tract ready.... Get good, striking tracts or none at all. But a touching gospel tract may be the seed of eternal life. Therefore do not go out without your tracts."

Never underestimate the power of a gospel tract. After George Whitefield read one called "The Life of God in the Soul of Man," he said, "God showed me I must be born again or be damned." He went on to pray: *Lord, if I am not a Christian, or if I am not a real one, for Jesus Christ's sake show me what Christianity is, that I may not be damned at last!* Then, as he wrote in his journal: "From that moment...did I know that I must become a new creature."

If you have never given out tracts, why not begin today? Leave them in a shopping cart, on a counter, in a public place or in the mail with your bills. Then each night as you shut your eyes to go to sleep, you will have something very special to pray about—that God will use the tract you put somewhere. You will also have a deep sense of satisfaction that you played a small part in carrying out the Great Commission to reach this dying world with the gospel of everlasting life.[2]

CHAPTER 11

Now Pray

AFTER HAVING SHARED the gospel with someone, we should diligently pray and intercede for them, asking the Holy Spirit to draw them to God. Our prayers, which are in agreement with the revealed will of God that all men should be saved, can be formidable weapons to deliver a soul from darkness and see them translated into the kingdom of light.

> Therefore I exhort first of all that supplications, *prayers, intercessions, and giving of thanks be made for all men*, for kings and all who are in authority, that we may lead a quiet and peaceable life in all godliness and reverence. For this is good and acceptable

in the sight of God our Savior, who *desires all men to be saved* and to come to the knowledge of the truth.

—1 TIMOTHY 2:1–4

The Lord is not slack concerning His promise, as some count slackness, but is longsuffering toward us, *not willing that any should perish but that all should come to repentance.*

—2 PETER 3:9

Epaphras, who is one of you, a bondservant of Christ, greets you, *always laboring fervently for you in prayers*, that you may *stand perfect and complete* in all the will of God.

—COLOSSIANS 4:12

Brethren, my heart's desire and *prayer to God* for Israel is *that they may be saved.*

—ROMANS 10:1

No one can come to Me unless *the Father who sent Me draws him*; and I will raise him up at the last day.

—JOHN 6:44

So *Abraham prayed to God*; and God healed Abimelech, his wife, and his female servants. Then they bore children.

—GENESIS 20:17

But *I have prayed for you*, that your faith should not fail; and when you have returned to Me, strengthen your brethren.

—LUKE 22:32

But, meanwhile, also prepare a guest room for me, for I trust that *through your prayers* I shall be granted to you.

—PHILEMON 22

I thank my God, *making mention of you always in my prayers*.

—PHILEMON 4

I thank God, whom I serve with a pure conscience, as my forefathers did, as without ceasing *I remember you in my prayers night and day*.

—2 TIMOTHY 1:3

My little children, for whom *I labor in birth* again until Christ is formed in you.

—GALATIANS 4:19

I have a good friend, Bishop Henry Madava, who is the pastor of one of Ukraine's largest churches in the city of Kiev. He is an African, born in Zimbabwe, but was sent by the Lord to the nation of Ukraine, where he started a church that has exploded in growth and now influences many nations for the gospel. When Henry was first confronted with the gospel, he was a university student who got into a debate with some Christians about their faith. But when he returned to his dormitory room after the confrontation, he found himself weeping for over two hours as the Holy Spirit began to work in his heart. Someone had been praying for him! He was gloriously converted and is now a leading apostolic figure in the twenty-first-century church.

With whom might we be sharing the gospel? What is their potential in the body of Christ? What is their future destiny? What amazing influence might they one day have in passing the gospel on to numerous others?

PRAY FOR CONVERTS AND PRAY FOR LABORERS

The Bible tells us to pray for laborers more times than it tells us to pray for converts, but both types of prayers are crucial in the kingdom of God. We are to pray for men to be saved, *and* we are to pray for laborers to be sent into the Master's harvest fields and bring the people in.

> Therefore I exhort first of all that *supplications, prayers, intercessions, and giving of thanks be made for all men*, for kings and all who are in authority, that we may lead a quiet and peaceable life in all godliness and reverence. For this is good and acceptable in the sight of God our Savior, who desires all men to be saved and to come to the knowledge of the truth.
>
> —1 TIMOTHY 2:1–4

> Then He said to His disciples, "The harvest truly is plentiful, but the laborers are few. Therefore *pray the Lord of the harvest to send out laborers* into His harvest."
>
> —MATTHEW 9:37–38

119

I pray for them. I do not pray for the world but for those whom You have given Me, for they are Yours.

—JOHN 17:9

I do not pray for these alone, but also for those who will believe in Me through their word; that they all may be one, as You, Father, are in Me, and I in You; that they also may be one in Us, that the world may believe that You sent Me.

—JOHN 17:20–21

But I say to you who hear: Love your enemies, do good to those who hate you, bless those who curse you, and *pray for those who spitefully use you*. To him who strikes you on the one cheek, offer the other also. And from him who takes away your cloak, do not withhold your tunic either. Give to everyone who asks of you. And from him who takes away your goods do not ask them back. And just as you want men to do to you, you also do to them likewise. But if you love those who love you, what credit is that to you? For even sinners love those who love them. And if you do good to those who do good to you, what credit is that to you? For even sinners do the same. And if you lend to those from whom you hope to receive back, what credit is that to you? For even sinners lend to sinners to receive as much back. But love your enemies, do good, and lend, hoping for nothing in return; and your reward will be great, and you will be sons of the Most High. For He is kind to the unthankful and evil. Therefore be merciful, just as your Father also is merciful.

—LUKE 6:27–36

You have heard that it was said, "You shall love your neighbor and hate your enemy." But I say to you, love your enemies, bless those who curse you, do good to those who hate you, and *pray for those who spitefully use you and persecute you*, that you may be sons of your Father in heaven; for He makes His sun rise on the evil and on the good, and sends rain on the just and on the unjust. For if you love those who love you, what reward have you? Do not even the tax collectors do the same? And if you greet your brethren only, what do you do more than others? Do not even the tax collectors do so? Therefore you shall be perfect, just as your Father in heaven is perfect.

—MATTHEW 5:43–48

PEOPLE FOR WHOM I AM PRAYING

❑ _____

❑ _____

❑ _____

❑ _____

❑ _____

❑ _____

❑ _____

❑ _____

❑ _____

❑ _____

❑ _____

❑ _____

❑ _____

CHAPTER 12

Savior or Sower

TRUE BELIEVERS IN Jesus Christ long to see the lost saved and brought into the kingdom, and they often put a great deal of pressure on themselves to see other people converted to the faith. But the simple truth is that no one can save another person except the Lord Jesus Himself. Only God can win souls. He is the *Savior*; we are just the *sowers*.

> I planted, Apollos watered, but *God gave the increase*. So then neither he who plants is anything, nor he who waters, but *God who gives the increase*. Now he who plants and he who waters are one, and each one will

receive his own reward according to his own labor.

—1 Corinthians 3:6–8

Our task and assignment from the Lord is to sow the seed of the gospel and believe that some of it will fall on good soil. Jesus instructed His disciples about the four kinds of soil on which the Word of God could fall.

The sower sows the word. And these are the *ones by the wayside* where the word is sown. When they hear, Satan comes immediately and takes away the word that was sown in their hearts. These likewise are the *ones sown on stony ground* who, when they hear the word, immediately receive it with gladness; and they have no root in themselves, and so endure only for a time. Afterward, when tribulation or persecution arises for the word's sake, immediately they stumble. Now these are *the ones sown among thorns*; they are the ones who hear the word, and the cares of this world, the deceitfulness of riches, and the desires for other things entering in choke the word, and it becomes unfruitful. But these are *the ones sown on good ground*, those who hear the word, accept it, and bear fruit: some thirtyfold, some sixty, and some a hundred.

—MARK 4:14–20

In each case, the sower himself could not determine the quality of the soil. His only task was to sow the seed. The people themselves—those who heard the Word of God—were depicted as the different types of soil. The sower was neutral, although he was diligent. Our task then is to be obedient sowers of the seed and leave the results of the harvest to the Lord. It is the hearers who bear the responsibility to respond to the Word in faith. Their faith, or lack of it, determines whether or not there will be fruit.

It is not the strength of the sower that determines the fruit of the harvest. Even the most feeble farmer can grow a crop. The power lies in the seed. Our Lord Jesus, through the Holy Spirit's work in the human heart, is the One who gives the increase. Some of us may sow, some of us may water, but God gives the increase! And as long as the earth is around, there will always be a harvest.

> While the earth remains,
> *Seedtime and harvest*,
> Cold and heat,
> Winter and summer,
> And day and night
> Shall not cease.
>
> —GENESIS 8:22

The Lord has promised us that His Word will do its work if we will be faithful to sow the seed into the hearts of people.

> For as the rain comes down, and the snow
>   from heaven,
> And do not return there,
> But water the earth,
> And make it bring forth and bud,
> That it may give seed to the sower
> And bread to the eater,
> *So shall My word be* that goes forth from
>   My mouth;
> It shall not return to Me void,
> But it shall accomplish what I please,
> And it shall prosper in the thing for which
>   I sent it.
>
> —ISAIAH 55:10–11

Now may He who supplies *seed to the sower*,
and bread for food, supply and multiply the
seed you have sown and increase the fruits
of your righteousness.
                           —2 CORINTHIANS 9:10

God can only water what we have sown. He
can only multiply the seed we sow. He can only
give the increase when there is something with
which He can work.

Cast your bread upon the waters,
For you will find it after many days.
                           —ECCLESIASTES 11:1

He who observes the wind will not sow,
And he who regards the clouds will not
    reap.
As you do not know what is the way of the
    wind,
Or how the bones grow in the womb of
    her who is with child,
So you do not know the works of God
    who makes everything.
In the morning sow your seed,
And in the evening do not withhold your
    hand;

> For you do not know which will prosper,
> Either this or that,
> Or whether both alike will be good.
> —ECCLESIASTES 11:4–6

Our task is to set the stage—to plant the seed by proclaiming the good news. Our job may be to move a person another notch up the scale of faith and bring them closer to God. If we will only be faithful to sow the powerful seed of the gospel, the Lord will do His part, and the harvest will come in. We must let the gospel do its work!

> For I am not ashamed of *the gospel of Christ, for it is the power of God* to salvation for everyone who believes, for the Jew first and also for the Greek.
>
> —ROMANS 1:16

Make a fresh commitment today to obey the command of Christ—to go and preach, to go and make disciples, to be a faithful witness both in your own Jerusalem and to the ends of the earth. Then, trust Him to bring in a harvest of souls.

We proclaim the gospel, we water it with love, we pray and intercede for the lost, and then God

128

gives a wonderful increase. We are the sowers—He is the Savior! Jesus is lifted up, and the Spirit draws people to God. Then they are born again, changed by the power of God, sealed by the Holy Spirit, and begin the process of becoming a faithful disciple of the Lord Jesus Christ.

CHAPTER 13

Making Disciples

I HAVE A FRIEND named Phil Cooke who is a producer in the media industry and lives in Los Angeles. Not long ago, he sent me the following e-mail:

> Recently, my daughter came home from high school shocked that her school friends had no idea what the cross meant. I was shopping at Christmas for a gift for my wife, and while at the jewelry counter, I watched a young couple looking at cross necklaces. As they looked, they came across a necklace with the figure of Jesus on the gold cross. The woman looked at the necklace and said:

> "That's really a beautiful cross necklace, but who's that little guy hanging on it?"

We are living in a world that does not know the story of Jesus. Although our country was founded on God and the truths of the Scriptures, we now live in a culture that has strayed far from its original purpose. People do not know the gospel. They have not heard the good news. They desperately need what we have to give—and they need more than just hearing John 3:16 quoted to them, or a simple prayer prayed to make them feel better. They need to be blasted out of the rock quarries of sin, delivered from the grip of darkness, and set free from the bondage of iniquity! They need an encounter with the living Christ. Although one motion picture's recent success has made a significant impact on people, they still need to be converted. They still need to be brought into the church and discipled. They still need to be born again and baptized. They need both conversion and transformation. They need the saving of their souls as well as the renewing of their minds. The early church preached for people to repent, be baptized, and receive the power of the Holy Spirit.

Jesus commissioned His followers to not only

go and preach the gospel, but also to go and make disciples! He expects disciplined believers—those who have been trained to follow Christ wherever He goes. New converts need to be brought into the church. We need to follow up on newly converted believers and connect them to a good local church for discipleship.

Here are some of the fundamental principles involved in making disciples:

1. People must make a clear confession of their faith in Jesus Christ and ask the Lord to forgive them of their sins and come into their hearts. New converts must make Jesus Christ the absolute Lord of their lives. He should not be just our Savior; He is also our Master and Lord.

2. There must be repentance from all forms of sin. New converts must be given an understanding of what sin is, as well as how to repent, change their ways, and turn from sin. Many churches now employ a weekend encounter retreat where new believers experience and encounter God in a very powerful way and receive personal ministry to help them be set free from sin, become rooted in Christ, and be planted in a church.

3. Every new believer needs a good local church where they can experience fellowship as well as accountability. In the local church there should be classes on the fundamentals of the faith, especially those listed in Hebrews 6.

4. A true disciple of Christ will have a good Bible as well as a practical understanding of how to read it and use it. A new disciple will need prayer and personal help in transitioning from the kingdom of darkness into the kingdom of light. A small Bible study group at this point can be a huge benefit for a new believer.

5. New converts are much like babies, and they need to be nurtured and cared for by committed, mature Christians. They need attention, time, tutoring, and training. They often need their hands held to get them to church, into fellowship, into the Bible, and into God. The mature believer should take the lead in contacting and following up on a new brother or sister and walk them through their first few months as a Christian.

CHAPTER 14

Someday

THE DAY IS fast approaching when supernatural events will begin to unfold and the purposes of God will ultimately be realized and fulfilled on the earth. Jesus Himself prophesied that this gospel would be preached in all the world as a witness to all nations before the end would come (Matt. 24:14).

These kind of apocalyptic days are coming upon this generation. Signs of the return of Christ seem to be impending. But this greatest of signs may be the key that brings fulfillment to all other End-Time prophecies. The gospel of the kingdom will be preached throughout the world. No doubt a great harvest of souls will ensue; even now the conversion rate of people coming to Christ is growing quickly. Many church growth analysts and missions experts forecast over one billion new converts to Christ in the next decade alone. Other Christian research groups are confirming these same gains in the kingdom of God over the next several years. Many theologians and students of Bible prophecy are sensing that perhaps the greatest spiritual harvest of humanity in a single generation may occur in our lifetime.

In 2003, evangelist Reinhard Bonnke held one of the largest Christian gatherings in history. Nearly two million people at one time were in attendance at his crusade in Nigeria, and over three million filled out cards expressing newfound faith in Christ. All this in only six days of ministry! Even today, a predominant portion of the continent of Africa is still experiencing a great wave of harvest, although millions more still need Christ.

Dr. Bill Bright once told me of meetings he held in Korea in which he personally spoke to over one million people at once. Some of the largest churches in the history of the world are in existence today. Dr. Cho's church in South Korea has a membership of hundreds of thousands of believers. Nigeria boasts churches that also number in the hundreds of thousands. Several churches in Latin America have broken the hundred-thousand-member barrier. Even American churches are growing larger than ever before, and church planting is spreading rapidly across the country and around the world. This is truly a time of great ingathering.

Modern technology is exponentially multiplying the efforts of churches and ministries as well. Digital video and Internet equipment are making an enormous global impact. People of all nations currently have access to the benefits of cyberspace and the kind of technology that may present every human being with the claims of the gospel of Jesus Christ in our lifetime. Even in the entertainment industry, movies such as *The Passion of the Christ* are giving people an extraordinary glimpse into the life and ministry of our Savior.

Twenty-first-century believers need to be prepared for the flood of souls that is beginning to pour into the kingdom of God. This harvest of people could nearly overwhelm unprepared local churches with a desperate cry for laborers. We will soon be like the disciples who had to call for their partners to help bring in the catch of fish.

Imagine this: the day may soon come when

literally everyone everywhere will be desperate to find help and refuge in God. In days like those predicted by Jesus Himself and in the Revelation of John, days of plague and pestilence, war and destruction, disaster and disease, people everywhere will cry out for "emergency" spiritual help. Similar to the days immediately following September 11, 2001 across America, people may be praying to God for help and going back to church in droves. If world events escalate as the prophets predict, they will dramatically awaken people to seek God and His divine intervention.

I recall once giving away pictures of our American missionary basketball team in the Philippines. These pictures had the gospel message printed on the back. The children of the barrios where we were playing literally jumped at us to pull them out of the hands of our team and workers. We were swarmed by children and young people grabbing at the "tracts" we were attempting to give away. All our plans for order quickly dissolved into chaos as the locals grabbed at the gospel souvenirs from the Christian American athletes.

Another ministry in our church involved handing out tracts in Russia, and these mission workers had the same experience as every piece of printed material was directly snatched out of their hands. Think of the coming days when every tract you own will be handed out, every Bible you have will be given away to desperate individuals, and every piece of the good news that people can get their hands on will be snatched up. Picture a time when people will be grabbing for these publications as if their very lives depended upon it.

From the homes of new church planters to the hallways of mega churches...from rented facilities to large church structures...from field meetings to stadium gatherings...visualize millions of people worldwide seeking the God of the Bible and calling upon the name of the Lord for salvation. Surely the days of the outpouring of the Spirit will one day coincide with cosmic events, and men will turn to the Lord by the thousands in every city, village, nation, and people group around the world. In such times, bold believers will be ready. We will have a word from God. We will have His divine love in our hearts. We will have the answers to people's questions. We will have the grace and anointing to lead people to Christ and see them discipled in the truth.

As we believe for those days to come, let us prepare ourselves now to begin to take advantage of the supernatural encounters the Holy Spirit brings across our paths. There are thousands of possibilities, hundreds of opportunities that will come our way—and scores of these occurrences present themselves daily. We should be prepared. We should position ourselves. We must take the initiative and be proactive. The Lord is already orchestrating these events in each of our lives. All we need to do is be confident and obedient to what He asks us to do.

Opportunities abound—dozens every day:

- While shopping
- During class
- At the coffee shop
- At the gas station
- In the drive-through
- At the cinema
- While walking through your neighborhood
- While watching your kid's ballgame
- When meeting a repairman at your house
- When you receive a wrong number
- When a telemarketer calls
- When making a bank deposit
- While waiting at a street corner
- As you garden in your yard
- At the driving range

140

- When exercising or working out
- At a reunion
- When riding in an elevator
- When eating at a restaurant
- When paying your parking fee
- When checking in at the airport
- When standing in line
- When sitting on your patio
- When riding your bicycle
- When walking your dog
- When washing your car
- When mowing your lawn
- When painting your house
- When picking up your mail
- When visiting a friend or neighbor
- On your way to church
- When you see an accident on the road

When you go to the mall, you are not just shopping. You should be scanning the needs of people around you. You should be searching the mall for divine opportunities. If you are a student, you are not just pursuing an education. That is just your "cover." You are on assignment to be a witness and love the people around you. If you are living in a particular neighborhood, you have been planted there by your heavenly Father to shine His light

141

into that part of the world. As you go through your day on the job, you are under cover—on assignment, incognito—a special agent for the kingdom of God, ready to be led by the very Spirit of Jesus to those who need Him the most.

CHAPTER 15

All Things Are Possible

A CHURCH OF 100 people probably has a core group of about 50 adults and young people who could be mobilized into a team ready to lead a bold gospel lifestyle. If 50 born-again believers would commit to sowing seeds of faith and love and sharing the gospel every week, think what could happen in their sphere of influence alone. They would sow hundreds of seeds of truth every week—thousands every year. If they each invited just one person a week to their church, that would be 2,600 invitations a year! If 100 churches in a given community with 50 mobilized believers would do the same, that would be 260,000 invitations per year, with maybe hundreds or even thousands of conversions taking place and many people finding abundant life in Christ.

I have challenged our church in Seattle to believe for 1,000 evangelists in our congregation to get serious about fulfilling the Great Commission of Jesus, doing the work of an evangelist and boldly sharing Christ with the people in our city. Although we have more than 4,000 people attending our church, with more being added each year through our new multisite congregational structure, we chose the number 1,000 because it is reachable and the number works easier for setting goals. If our 1,000 evangelists hand out an invitation to our church every day, that would be 365,000 invitations in one year. Most research tells us that 1 to 5 percent of those contacted will respond. That would mean that at least 3,650 people could respond, maybe even come to church, and many of those could get saved. And that is just our church alone!

Let's say that ten other churches do what we are doing; that would raise the calculation into millions of contacts, and into tens of thousands of potential converts. If that same action were taken in each of the states in our nation, those numbers would be multiplied by fifty, and the total of people potentially touched and reached in America alone would be 180 million, with 1.8 million becoming born again!

If all those numbers begin to exponentially multiply and continue over a period of just a few years, the possibilities are staggering! Conversions to Christ would begin to sweep from coast to coast and border to border in a major spiritual awakening. If it were to take place around the world in every nation, the results would boggle the human mind. This would be regarded as a primary revival and a twenty-first-century Great Awakening! And yet this kind of spiritual renewal is only a few conversations away from our grasp.

We need to simply talk about God, bless others around us, mention the name of the Lord, pray for the needs of others, invite people to church, and open the possibility of conversations that might lead to regeneration. This is possible. This is a reachable goal and a very viable achievement. Every one of us can do it. We may start small and simple, sharing with just a few people over a short period of time, but if we are faithful and persistent, the Lord will open up more and more doors for us to share the gospel with others.

I have had the privilege of sharing with presidents of the United States, other assorted politicians, star athletes, and successful businesspeople. It was exhilarating to be a part of sowing seed and watering it in their hearts. But I have also prayed with the homeless and the unknown, the stranger and the needy. People of all backgrounds need the Lord, and they need you to speak up and tell them the good news. If I can do it, I know you can! The Lord who calls us will be faithful to help.

After I told my son, Judah, about my high-school experiences and how I regretted not taking a stronger stand for Christ in a public way, he determined to do things differently in his senior year of high school. In obedience to the Holy Spirit's leading and with my encouragement, he made several passionate statements to his classmates. On the very first day of school that year, he stood on a chair in the middle of a packed cafeteria and boldly told his classmates that he was a Christian. He invited everyone to join him for a lunchtime Bible study that he was starting that week. Although he was later reprimanded by an assistant principal, he had already made the statement that was needed for the seed of the gospel to be planted. He later led several of his varsity

146

basketball teammates to the Lord, some of whom are still in our church today.

By the end of that climactic school year, Judah had organized a major gathering of young people in the school football stadium right before graduation. It was called "Last Stand," and over five hundred kids attended, with more than fifty making commitments to Christ. Judah Smith is now our generation pastor, reaching nearly one thousand young people every week in the Seattle area. He leads conferences, writes books, trains interns, sends workers to campuses, and is making disciples of a new generation. He has spoken to literally hundreds of thousands of young people around America and other nations already in his short lifetime.

Judah may be one of the many new prototypes for the twenty-first-century church—a church that boldly speaks up and proclaims the good news everywhere it goes. In those few seconds or minutes when God opens the door, lives can be changed. In one moment of time, *we* can affect a soul for eternity. Join the revolution, and make a difference in someone's life in just 60 seconds!

NOTES

INTRODUCTION

1. Sujo John, *Do You Know Where You Are Going? One Man's Story of September 11 and the Saving Grace of Jesus Christ* (New York: Lantern Books, 2002).

2. "Husband, Anderson 'Fervently Lived for God,'" *Baptist Messenger,* www. baptistmessenger .com/Issue/030213/5.html (accessed May 18, 2004).

3. "President Addresses Nation on Space Shuttle Columbia," Office of the Press Secretary, February 1, 2003: www.whitehouse.gov/news /releases/2003/02/20030201-2.html (accessed May 18, 2004).

CHAPTER 4
REDEEMING THE TIME

1. William Fay, *Share Jesus Without Fear*, (Nashville, TN: Broadman & Holman Publishers, 1999).

CHAPTER 7
WHEN YOU CAN TAKE SOME TIME

1. Fay, *Share Jesus Without Fear*.

CHAPTER 10
PROCLAIMING THE GOSPEL

1. Ray Comfort, *The Evidence Bible: Irrefutable Evidence for the Thinking Mind* (Gainesville, FL: Bridge-Logos Publishers, 2001), footnotes for Revelation 22:2.

2. Ibid., footnotes for 1 Corinthians 9:22.

Appendix A

Twenty-first-Century Gospel Resources

Fresh ideas of things to give people

- Web site addresses

- "Touch cards": In 1991, we invented and designed the first touch cards for our pastor's church in Portland, Oregon, and we now use the same concept in our church in Seattle. A touch card is usually of a different shape and size from a typical business card, and it might include a map to a church, photos, Web site, and e-mail information as well as a space for a personal message. Our slogan for using touch cards is: "Touching our city, one person at a time." You can see an example at the end of this appendix.

- The *Jesus* Film on video (now in over eight hundred languages and seen by over five billion people)

- A worship CD

- A preaching CD

151

FROM ZERO TO ETERNITY IN 60 SECONDS FLAT

- A dynamic Christian DVD or video

- A best-selling Christian book

- A classic Christian book

- A Christian booklet

- Excerpts from the Bible or New Testament set in cool or unusual fonts

- Your printed personal testimony

- The printed personal testimony of someone else

- Food: groceries or a hot meal

- Clothing: a warm coat or new shoes

- A blanket or an umbrella

- Money (use caution here and be led by the Holy Spirit)

- A Bible

- "The Four Spiritual Laws," perhaps the greatest gospel tool of all time

Just as there are physical laws that govern the physical universe, so are there spiritual laws which govern your relationship with God

 God LOVES you and offers a wonderful PLAN for your life.

God's Love

"God so loved the world that He gave His one and only Son, that whoever believes in Him shall not perish, but have eternal life" (John 3:16 NIV).

God's Plan

[Christ speaking] "I came that they might have life, and might have it abundantly" [that it might be full and meaningful] (John 10:10).

Why is it that most people are not experiencing the abundant life? Because...

 Man is SINFUL and SEPARATED from God. Therefore, he cannot know and experience God's love and plan for his life.

Man Is Sinful

"All have sinned and fall short of the glory of God" (Romans 3:23).

Man was created to have fellowship with God; but, because of his stubborn self-will, he chose to go his own independent way, and fellowship with God was broken. This self-will, characterized by an attitude of active rebellion or passive indifference, is an evidence of what the Bible calls sin.

Man Is Separated

"The wages of sin is death" [spiritual separation from God] (Romans 6:23).

This diagram illustrates that God is holy and man is sinful. A great gulf separates the two. The arrows illustrate that man is continually trying to reach God and the abundant life through his own efforts, such as a good life, philosophy, or religion - but he inevitably fails. The third law explains the only way to bridge this gulf...

 Jesus Christ is God's ONLY provision for man's sin. Through Him you can know and experience God's love and plan for your life.

He Died in Our Place

"God demonstrates His own love toward us, in that while we were yet sinners, Christ died for us" (Romans 5:8).

He Rose From the Dead
"Christ died for our sins...He was buried...He was raised on the third day, according to the Scriptures...He appeared to Peter, then to the twelve. After that He appeared to more than five hundred..." (1 Corinthians 15:3-6).

He Is the Only Way to God
"Jesus said to him, 'I am the way, and the truth, and the life; no one comes to the Father, but through Me'" (John 14:6).

This diagram illustrates that God has bridged the gulf which separates us from Him by sending His Son, Jesus Christ, to die on the cross in our place to pay the penalty for our sins. It is not enough just to know these three laws...

 We must individually RECEIVE Jesus Christ as Savior and Lord; then we can know and experience God's love and plan for our lives.

We Must Receive Christ
"As many as received Him, to them He gave the right to become children of God, even to those who believe in His name" (John 1:12)

We Receive Christ Through Faith
"By grace you have been saved through faith; and that not of yourselves, it is the gift of God; not as a result of works, that no one should boast" (Ephesians 2:8,9).

We Receive Christ by Personal Invitation
[Christ speaking] "Behold, I stand at the door and knock; if any one hears My voice and opens the door, I will come in to him" (Revelation 3:20).

Receiving Christ involves turning to God from self (repentance) and trusting Christ to come into our lives to forgive our sins and to make us what He wants us to be. Just to agree intellectually that Jesus Christ is the Son of God and that He died on the cross for our sins is not enough. Nor is it enough to have an emotional experience. We receive Jesus Christ by faith, as an act of the will.

These two circles represent two kinds of lives. Which best describes your life?

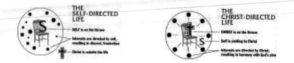

Which circle would you like to have represent your life?

The following explains how you can receive Christ

You Can Receive Christ Right Now by Faith Through Prayer
(Prayer is talking to God)

God knows your heart and is not so concerned with your words as He is with the attitude of your heart. The following is a suggested prayer:

"Lord Jesus, I need You. Thank You for dying on the cross for my sins. I open the door of my life and receive You as my Savior and Lord. Thank You for forgiving my sins and giving me eternal life. Take control of the throne of my life. Make me the kind of person You want me to be."

Does this prayer express the desire of your heart? If it does, I invite you to pray this prayer right now, and Christ will come into your life, as He promised.

How to Know That Christ Is in Your Life
Did you receive Christ into your life by sincerely praying the suggested prayer? According to His promise in Revelation 3:20, where is Christ right now in relation to you? Christ said that He would come into your life. Would He mislead you? On what authority do you know that God has answered your prayer? (The trustworthiness of God Himself and His Word.)

The Bible Promises Eternal Life
"The witness is this, that God has given us eternal life, and this life is in His Son. He who has the Son has the life; he who does not have the Son of God does not have life. These things I have written to you who believe in the name of the Son of God, in order that you may know that you have eternal life" (1 John 5:11-13).

Thank God often that Christ is in your life and that He will never leave you (Hebrews 13:5). You can know on the basis of His promise that Christ lives in you and that you have eternal life from the very moment you invite Him in. He will not deceive you.

Do Not Depend on Feelings
The promise of God's Word, the Bible - not our feelings - is our authority. The Christian lives by faith (trust) in the trustworthiness of God Himself and His Word. This train diagram illustrates the relationship among fact (God and His Word), faith (our trust in God and His Word), and feeling (the result of our faith and obedience) (John 14:21).

To be transported by a jet, we must place our faith in the trustworthiness of the aircraft and the pilot who flies it. Our feelings of confidence or fear do not affect the ability of the jet to transport us, though they do affect how much we enjoy the trip. In the same way, we as Christians do not depend on feelings or emotions, but we place our faith (trust) in the trustworthiness of God and the promises of His Word.

Now That You Have Received Christ...

The moment that you received Christ by faith, as an act of the will, many things happened, including the following:

1.) Christ came into your life (Revelation 3:20 ; Colossians 1:27).
2.) Your sins were forgiven (Colossians 1:14).
3.) You became a child of God (John 1:12).
4.) You received eternal life (John 5:24).
5.) You began the great adventure for which God created you (John 10:10; 2 Corinthians 5:17 ; 1 Thessalonians 5:18).

Can you think of anything more wonderful that could happen to you than receiving Christ? Would you like to thank God in prayer right now for what He has done for you? By thanking God, you demonstrate your faith.

Suggestions for Christian Growth

Spiritual growth results from trusting Jesus Christ. "The righteous man shall live by faith" (Galatians 3:11). A life of faith will enable you to trust God increasingly with every detail of your life, and to practice the following:

Go to God in prayer daily (John 15:7).
Read God's Word daily (Acts 17:11); begin with the Gospel of John.
Obey God moment by moment (John 14:21).
Witness for Christ by your life and words (Matthew 4:19; John 15:8).
Trust God for every detail of your life (1 Peter 5:7).
Holy Spirit - allow Him to control and empower your daily life and witness (Galatians 5:16,17; Acts 1:8).

Fellowship in a Good Church

God's Word instructs us not to forsake "the assembling of ourselves together" (Hebrews 10:25). Several logs burn brightly together; but put one aside on the cold hearth and the fire goes out. So it is with your relationship with other Christians. If you do not belong to a church, do not wait to be invited. Take the initiative; call the pastor of a nearby church where Christ is honored and His Word is preached. Start this week, and make plans to attend regularly.

Special Materials Are Available for Christian Growth

If you have come to Christ personally through this presentation of the gospel, helpful materials for Christian growth are available to you. Visit www.newlifepubs.com. Do you still have questions about Jesus? Visit www.whoisjesus-really.com. *You will want to share this important discovery*

Local Church Gospel Tract

(Diagram of The City Church gospel tract: "The Truth Is . . . ," used with permission)

two everybody knows there's something wrong

In a world full of war, terror, sickness and death, all of us recognize the existence and reality of evil.

"And lead us not into temptation; but deliver us from evil." - Matthew 6:13

"For out of the heart proceed evil thoughts, murders, adulteries, fornications, thefts, false witness, blasphemies." - Matthew 15:19

three: everybody has heard of Jesus Christ

The Person who divided modern history in half is widely recognized as the most influential individual who ever lived. Jesus Christ was a real historical figure who lived and died and has impacted millions of people's lives for more than two thousand years.

"For God so loved the world that He gave His only begotten Son, that whoever believes in Him should not perish but have everlasting life." - John 3:16

"and you shall call His name Jesus, for He shall save His people from their sins." Matthew 1:21

"[God] has appointed a day on which He will judge the world in righteousness by the Man whom He has ordained. He has given assurance of this to all by raising Him from the dead." - Acts 17:30-31

four: everybody needs forgiveness

All of us have done things we are ashamed of. All of us sense the need for forgiveness for weaknesses, faults, failures and wrongdoings.

"All have sinned and fall short of the glory of God." - Romans 3:23

"When Jesus saw their faith, He said to the paralytic, "Son, your sins are forgiven you." - Mark 2:5

"Therefore let it be known to you, brethren, that through this Man is preached to you the forgiveness of sins; and by Him everyone who believes is justified." - Acts 13:38-39

prayer of salvation

Dear God - I need your help. I believe that Jesus Christ is the son of God and rose from the dead. I ask you to forgive me of my sins and come into my heart. Be my Lord and Savior. Amen

Appendix B

Recommended Web Sites

The City Church
www.thecity.org

Global Pastors Network
www.globalpastorsnetwork.org

The *Jesus* Film
www.jesusfilm.org

Campus Crusade
www.campuscrusade.org

Navigators
www.navigators.org

American Bible Society
www.americanbible.org

Generation Ministries
www.generationchurch.org

Appendix C

Evangelistic Books

Great books on evangelism

Anderson, Ken. *A Coward's Guide to Witnessing*.

Covell, Jim, Karen Covell, and Victorya Michaels Rogers. *How to Talk About Jesus Without Freaking Out*. Sisters, OR: Multnomah Publishers Inc., 2000.

Estes, Marc. *Jesus Today*. Portland, OR: City Bible Publishing, 2001.

Fay, William. *Share Jesus Without Fear*. Nashville, TN: Broadman & Holman Publishers, 1999.

Hybels, Bill, and Mark Mittelberg. *Becoming a Contagious Christian*. Grand Rapids, MI: Zondervan Corp., 1996.

Great books to give away to seekers

Bright, Bill. *Ten Basic Steps*. Available online through www.campuscrusade.com

―――. *Transferable Concepts*. Available online through www.campuscrusade.com

Colson, Charles. *Loving God*. Grand Rapids, MI: Zondervan Corp., 1997.

Estes, Marc. *Jesus Today*. Portland, OR: City Bible Publishing, 2001.

Graham, Dr. Billy. *Just As I Am: The Autobiography of Billy Graham*. New York, NY: HarperCollins Publishers, 1999.

Graham, Franklin. *The Name*. Nashville, TN: Thomas Nelson, 2002.

McDowell, Josh. *The New Evidence That Demands a Verdict*. Nashville, TN: Nelson Reference, 1999.

Wilkinson, Bruce. *The Prayer of Jabez*. Sisters, OR: Multnomah Publishers, 2000.

OTHER RESOURCES
BY WENDELL SMITH

Books/Booklets

Great Faith; Roots of Character; The Divine Economy; God Can Still Bless America; Raising Faith-Filled Kids

"Rhema Cards"

Daily Prayer Card; Discovering the Will of God; Healing of Infirmity; Holiness; Holy Spirit Anointing; Identity in Christ; Joy Is a Choice; My Body—Keeping It Healthy; No Fear; Prosperity With a Purpose; Purity; Search Me; Speak to Your Mountain; Strength; Victory Over Enemies; Week in the Word: Bible Reading Plan; Wisdom and the Will of God

DVDs

Dragonslayer; From Now On—Caught Between a Rock and a Reed; Shut the Doors and Open the Windows—I Want the Men to Pray

Conferences

Generation Church Conference; Prosperity With a Purpose Conference; Global Strategy Conference

For more information on The City Church, any of the products, or conferences listed here, please contact:

The City Church
9051 132nd Avenue NE
Kirkland, WA 98033
Phone: 1-800-304-CITY
Fax: 425-889-8940
Web site: www.thecity.org

Strang Communications, the publisher of both Charisma House and *Charisma* magazine, wants to give you a FREE SUBSCRIPTION to our award-winning magazine.

Since its inception in 1975, *Charisma* magazine has helped thousands of Christians stay connected with what God is doing worldwide.

Within its pages you will discover in-depth reports and the latest news from a Christian perspective, biblical health tips, global events in the body of Christ, personality profiles, and so much more. Join the family of *Charisma* readers who enjoy feeding their spirit each month with miracle-filled testimonies and inspiring articles that bring clarity, provoke prayer, and demand answers.

To claim your **3 free issues** of *Charisma,* send us your name and address to: Charisma 3 Free Issue Offer, 600 Rinehart Road, Lake Mary, FL 32746. Or you may call 1-800-829-3346 and ask for Offer # 93FREE. This offer is only valid in the USA.

www.charismamag.com